HANDBOOK OF RECREATIONAL GAMES

COMPILED BY NEVA L. BOYD

With a New Introduction by Ruth Austin

DOVER PUBLICATIONS, INC.
New York

Published in Canada by General Publishing Company, Ltd., 30 Lesmill Road, Don Mills, Toronto, Ontario.
Published in the United Kingdom by Constable and Company, Ltd., 10 Orange Street, London, WC 2.

This Dover edition, first published in 1975, is a republication of the work originally published in 1945 by H. T. FitzSimons Company, Inc., Chicago under the title *Handbook of Games*. A new Introduction has been written especially for this edition by Ruth Austin.

International Standard Book Number: 0-486-23204-2
Library of Congress Catalog Card Number: 75-13385

Manufactured in the United States of America
Dover Publications, Inc.
180 Varick Street
New York, N.Y. 10014

Introduction

This reprint of *Handbook of Games* by Neva L. Boyd again makes available a useful collection of carefully selected games which was compiled by Miss Boyd in her early years of teaching. Former pupils, concerned when *Handbook of Games* went out of print several years ago, are delighted to know that this reprint will further perpetuate Miss Boyd's work.

Neva Boyd was an internationally known educator in group leadership, childhood education, recreation and social group work. Her contributions began with her organization of the Chicago Training School for Playground Workers in 1911, and continued with her direction of the Department of Recreation in the Chicago School of Civics and Philanthropy from 1914 to 1920, and with her own Recreation Training School, conducted in Chicago's Hull House from 1921 to 1927. In the Fall of 1927 her courses in recreation became a part of the Sociology Department of Northwestern University where Miss Boyd taught play theory, leadership, group organization and other related subjects until her retirement in 1941, when she became consultant to the Activity Therapy Program in the State Schools of Illinois under the Department of Welfare. From that time until her death in 1963 she continued to teach, giving special courses in the purposeful use of play activities as a means of enhancing and improving social relationships.

Early in her teaching career the response of children in play programs led Neva Boyd to her far-visioned thesis that there is an important relationship between play and the social education of children. Throughout her long and distinguished teaching career, and in her consultation and in-service training programs conducted for a diverse range of groups and organizations all over the country, Miss Boyd combined theory with practice. She gave joyful zest to teaching games, folk dancing and dramatics, always stressing that such activities should be valued for their intrinsic good—not for external rewards—and that when leader and participants engaged both psychologically and physically in the right activities, there would be improved social relationships.

While the promotion of good play activities for normal children and adults was always of interest to Miss Boyd, she perceived early

INTRODUCTION

in her teaching that appropriate play activities could be used as an effective way of communicating with hard-to-reach individuals. Consequently, long before the benefits to be derived from "recreation therapy" came to be widely recognized, Miss Boyd and numerous of her students had demonstrated both the educational and the therapeutic values of play with groups in specialized settings, such as Chicago Children's Memorial Hospital, some Illinois Veterans' Hospitals, Chicago State Hospital, Lincoln Illinois State School for Retarded, and the State School for Girls in Geneva, Illinois.

Handbook of Games was among the earliest of Miss Boyd's writings, which included hitherto unpublished compilations of folk dances and other social activities collected in this country and abroad. An interesting companion-piece for those who wish to learn more about Miss Boyd's theories regarding play and games is *Play and Game Theory in Group Work, a Collection of Papers by Neva Leona Boyd.* Paul Simon, Editor, the Jane Addams Graduate School of Social Work. This book is available from The Bookstore, University of Illinois at Circle Campus, Box 4348, Chicago, Illinois 60680.

RUTH AUSTIN

Contents

FOREWORD 6

PURSUIT AND ESCAPE GAMES 7

HOPPING AND JUMPING GAMES 23

THROWING AND CATCHING GAMES 34

THROWING AT A MARK GAMES 39

BOUNCING BALL GAMES 48

PULLING AND PUSHING GAMES 58

KICKING GAMES 60

STRIKING GAMES 62

HIDING GAMES 67

RACING GAMES 74

SENSE GAMES 76

INTELLECTUAL GAMES 86

DRAMATIC GAMES 105

TRICK GAMES 108

WITCH GAMES 111

GAMES REQUIRING VOLUNTARY CONTROL OF
   IMPULSES 114

CONTEST FOR PLACES AND SIMILAR GAMES 116

MISCELLANEOUS GAMES 121

INDEX 125

Foreword

Several hundred tried and tested games that have brought enjoyment to children and adults, generation after generation, have been compiled in this collection for the purpose of making them accessible to parents, teachers, and other lovers of games.

The educational value for so-called normal children of games dynamically played is unquestioned; their therapeutic value for hospitalized children has been demonstrated beyond doubt; their use as therapy in the treatment of mental patients has proved effective; and their corrective value in the re-education of problem youth has been repeatedly demonstrated in schools and custodial institutions.

While the descriptions of the games in this collection are confined to the concise rules, which are essential as orderly guides and as helps to the maintenance of stability, the vitality of the game lies in the creative process of playing it. Because of its dynamic character, the playing of a game is never twice alike, regardless of the number of repetitions or the stability of the membership of the playing group. This is why the old games can be played repeatedly with increasing satisfaction.

The discipline of making judgments, often instantaneously, and of acting upon them within a static frame of reference i.e., the verbalized rules, is unique to the playing of games. While the game is an imaginatively set up structure into which the players project themselves psychologically, they act consistently with the demands of the situation, and thereby subject themselves to self-imposed discipline, which involves many aspects of social behavior.

The omission of any suggestion of specific values as related to particular games in this compilation is intentional. Games are the organized accumulation of play-behavior, and since play-behavior is centered largely in the thalamic region of the nervous system, and is therefore closely related to the outside world, every player has access to the stimulation of the dynamic process, and of necessity gets values out of his own experience. Because this is true, any attempts to set up values as goals for the players would tend to defeat the possibility of their experiencing these values spontaneously.

The classification of the games as made, may be of help in getting variety, particularly in the organization of play programs for children, but it is in no sense scientific, and little can be said for its merit beyond the fact that, for the most part, it suggests the predominantly objective behavior the particular game calls forth, and therefore indirectly suggests variety to the teacher.

NEVA L. BOYD.

Pursuit and Escape Games

Over Bridges and Roads

This is a tag game played on roller skates and on a hard surface on which a large diagram may be drawn, with sufficient spaces between the bodies of water for the skaters to keep to the roads and bridges, and avoid getting into the water (see diagram).

The skaters may rest on the letter "G," wherever written, and while there, may not be tagged; but since only one may rest on a letter at the same time, and since the most recent comer has precedence, the earlier arrival must give way to him.

One player is *It* until he tags someone who is not resting on a letter "G" or until he sees someone's skates touching the water.

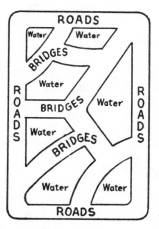

Arrow Chase

The players are divided into two teams, each of which chooses a captain. While one team blinds, the other starts off on a run. The captain and one or two other members, who have pieces of chalk, draw arrows in plain sight but not necessarily readily seen by the other team. The arrows should all point in the direction the leaders are taking, and should be drawn every ten or fifteen feet.

After blinding for the time agreed upon, which is in relation to the distance the leaders plan to run, the blinders start off. They must follow the arrows in their efforts to overtake the leaders before their

7

course leads them back to the starting place. The players do not run for goal, as they do in many somewhat similar games.

Prisoner's Base

The players are divided into two teams—*A* and *B*, and stand behind their own goal lines at either end of a field one hundred or more feet long (see diagram). The game starts by one player giving a dare by running out into the field. Let us say an *A* player does this. A *B* player may run out to tag him, a second *A* may come out to tag *B*, whereupon the first *A* must return to goal, since one may tag only those *who came out before he did.*

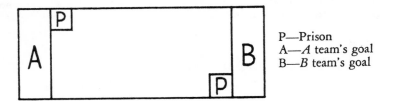

P—Prison
A—*A* team's goal
B—*B* team's goal

When a player is tagged, he is put in prison and must keep one foot anchored in the prison until a second prisoner is brought in. The new prisoner must now stand with one foot in the prison, but the first one may stand outside the prison, provided he keeps one hand joined with the new prisoner. Thereafter the last prisoner brought into prison must anchor the line of prisoners by keeping one foot in the prison, while the other prisoners may stretch out in a line in the order in which they were captured.

Prisoners may be rescued by their teammates' running through the opponents' field and getting one foot in their goal or by running into their field and reaching the end prisoner farthest from the prison without being tagged. In either case, this end prisoner must be rescued first. Both the rescuer and the prisoner may go back to their own goal in safety. Also, any player who makes a run completely encircling both fields and prisons without being tagged, thereby frees all the prisoners belonging to his side.

The object of the game is to get all opponents in prison at one time.

Note: This game can be played only by those who play fairly and who are alert enough to know who came out before them. Also, only experienced players and those who play an offensive game can play the game successfully.

Stealing Sticks

The players divide into two teams—*A* and *B*. A space a hundred or more feet long is divided into two equal fields, at the end of each of which is a goal about three feet square (see diagram), in which each player places a stick. Each of the teams has a prison also located at the end of the field.

The object of the game is to steal all the opponents' sticks or to get all their players in prison at one time. The players try to run through the opponents' field and to get one foot in the goal containing the sticks without being tagged. If a player succeeds, he may bring back a stick or a prisoner; and on this return trip he may not be tagged.

Should a player be tagged when attempting to steal a stick, he is put in the opponents' prison and must stand with one foot anchored in the prison until another prisoner is brought in. The new prisoner takes the place of the first one and must keep one foot anchored in the prison, but the first prisoner may stand outside, provided he keeps one hand joined with the new prisoner. Thereafter, the last prisoner brought in must anchor the line of prisoners by keeping one foot in the prison while the others may stretch out in a line in the order in which they were captured.

A prisoner may be rescued in one of three ways: by a player running through the opponents' field and getting one foot in the goal containing the sticks or in the prison; or by reaching the prisoner farthest from the prison without being tagged. Thus the prisoner who was tagged first is first to be rescued. Both the rescuer and the prisoner may go safely back to their own goal.

The game ends when all the players of one side are in prison or when all the sticks of one side have been stolen.

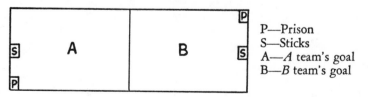

P—Prison
S—Sticks
A—*A* team's goal
B—*B* team's goal

Drop the Handkerchief

The players stand in a circle with one player as *It,* who runs around outside the circle and drops the handkerchief behind one of the players. That player picks it up and tries to tag the first player before he can get around the circle and back to his pursuer's place. If he is tagged, he is *It* again; if not, his pursuer becomes *It.* However, if the player behind whom the handkerchief is dropped fails to discover it before *It* runs completely round the circle and picks it up, that player goes into the "mush pot" (the center of the circle) and remains there until a second player is made to go in, whereupon the first one is released and joins the circle again.

When the handkerchief is dropped behind a player, the others pretend not to see it.

Drop the Handkerchief in Couples

Couples stand in a circle with adjacent hands joined with partner. One couple is *It*. This couple run outside the circle and drop the handkerchief behind another couple and continue running round the circle. The other couple pick up the handkerchief, provided they discover it (the other players avoid giving them any help), and immediately give chase, trying to tag the fleeing couple before they get round the circle and back to the vacancy created by their pursuers. Should the couple who is *It* be tagged, they continue to be *It;* if not, the pursuers are *It*.

Should the couple behind whom the handkerchief is dropped fail to discover it, the couple who dropped it pick it up and drop it behind another couple.

Unless the taggers have their hands joined when the tagging takes place they continue to be *It;* and if the other couple release their hold and one is tagged, he and his partner are *It*.

Three Deep

With the exception of a runner and a tagger, the players stand in a circle two by two, one behind the other, facing the center. Both the runner and the tagger must run outside the circle. The runner runs around and darts in front of a couple, making three in a line. The third player immediately becomes the runner.

In case the runner is tagged before he gets in front of a couple, he becomes tagger and the tagger becomes the runner. The runner must not run across in front of a couple but he may dart in from either side.

Two Deep

A runner and a chaser are chosen, and all the other players stand in a single circle. The runner, pursued by the chaser, runs around the circle and darts in front of any player he chooses, thereby making that player the runner. When the chaser succeeds in tagging the runner or the person in front of whom he has stopped before that person starts to run, their roles are instantly reversed.

Both the runner and the chaser must run outside the circle.

Snatch the Handkerchief

The players divide into two equal groups and stand in lines facing each other, fifteen or twenty feet apart. Beginning at opposite ends, the players number consecutively, so that there are corresponding numbers in each line, thus:

1 2 3 4 5
5 4 3 2 1

Equidistant between the two lines, a blunt stick about twelve inches long is stuck in the ground or stood upright in a small box. A handkerchief is hung over the top of the stick. (An Indian club might well be used for this purpose.)

The leader calls a number, and the two players having these numbers run forward and try to snatch the handkerchief. The one who succeeds in getting it tries to get back to his own place in his line with it before the other player can tag him. Neither one may be tagged until he has touched the handkerchief.

Two points are scored for the side whose player gets back to his place with the handkerchief safely, and one point is scored for the side whose player tags successfully.

Last Couple Out

An odd number of players is required for the game. The players line up in couples, one behind the other, the head couple being three or four feet behind the odd player, who is catcher. All face in the same direction. When the catcher calls "Last couple out," the partners of the last couple in the line separate and run, one on either side of the line of players toward the head of the line and past the catcher. Their aim is to encircle the catcher and join hands before he can tag either of them. They may run as far afield as they wish in doing so. The catcher may not turn his head to see where the runners are nor may he chase them until they are even with him. If one of the players is caught, he and the catcher form a couple and stand at the head of the line, and the other player becomes catcher. If neither of the runners is caught, they stand at the head of the line, and the same player continues as catcher.

Black and White, or Day and Night

The players are divided into two teams, one called, "Black" and the other "White." The teams stand facing each other in two lines five or more feet apart and equidistant between two goals approximately thirty feet apart. The leader stands at one end of the lines and tosses up a block painted white on three sides and black on three sides. If the block falls with the white uppermost, the Whites run for their goal pursued by the Blacks, who try to tag as many as possible. All who are tagged join the taggers' side, and the game continues as before.

The players determine the number of times the game shall be played. The side having the greatest number of players at the end wins.

Crooks and Cranes

This is played the same as *Black and White*, with the exception that the teams are "Crooks" and "Cranes," and the leader calls "Crooks" or "Cranes," drawing out the "cr" to deceive the players.

Couple Tag

I.   The players form in couples, and with hands joined run freely about the room. One player is runner, and the other chaser. To avoid being tagged by the chaser, the runner may join hands with either member of any couple, whereupon that player's partner becomes runner. However, if the chaser succeeds in tagging the runner, he himself becomes runner, and the runner becomes chaser.

II.   If there is an odd number of players, the game may be played with one person as *It*. The couples run to escape *It*, who tries to join hands with one of the players. If he succeeds, that player's partner becomes *It*.

Save a Friend Tag

One player is chosen to be tagger. Any object that can be easily passed from one player to another is given to one of the group. The tagger tries to tag the player who has the object, and all the others co-operate to save their friend when he is being pursued, by taking the object from him and running away with it. All must help to keep the object moving from one to another, as this makes it more difficult for the tagger. If the tagger succeeds in tagging a player who has the object, that player hands the object to another in the group and immediately becomes tagger.

Black Tom

One of the players volunteers to be tagger; the others line up on one of two parallel goals, such as the curbs of a street, approximately sixty feet apart. The tagger stands midway between the two goals and calls "Black Tom, Black Tom, Blue Tom," or any color he chooses to name at the end, in such a way as to induce the players to step forward before he calls "Black Tom, Black Tom, Black Tom!" and thus be made a tagger. When the tagger calls "Black Tom" three times in succession, all the players must run for the opposite goal, and the tagger tags as many as possible. Those tagged become taggers, and the game continues until all are tagged.

I Send

Two captains choose sides and line up their teams on goal lines about thirty feet apart with side boundaries fixed if necessary. The last chooser has the first turn. This captain says, "I send Mary (any player of his own team) after Ruth (anyone he chooses from the opposite team)." Ruth then must try to run to the opposite goal without being tagged by Mary. If she succeeds, she may return to her own team; but if tagged, she must join Mary's team. In any case, the captain of the other team then sends out a player. The captain may send himself or may challenge the captain of the opponents' side. If a captain is caught, he appoints another captain for his side. The team with the largest number of players when the game ends wins.

Eagle and the Birds

All the players, with the exception of the eagle, sit on the floor or ground in a circle. The eagle gives each of the players the name of a bird, then seats himself in the center, and calls the name of any bird he chooses. That bird runs around outside the circle pursued by the eagle, who must start by running through the opening where the bird sat. If the eagle catches the bird before he gets back to his place in the circle, the bird becomes the eagle; if not, the same player continues as eagle.

Numbers Change in Couples

Equal numbers of couples stand on opposite goal lines, thirty or more feet apart. The couples in each line number off consecutively and then move about to mix up the numbers. Either one of these couples, or an odd couple volunteers to be tagger. This couple stands midway between the goals and calls one of the assigned numbers. The couples having that number must immediately run to the opposite goal while the taggers try to tag one of them. All partners must keep their hands joined or must rejoin them immediately should they be released when tagging or running for goals. Any couple that fails to do so, must exchange places with the taggers even though they may not have been tagged.

As the game progresses, two couples having the same number may be at the same goal, but even so, both run to the opposite goal when their number is called.

Stiff Legged Tag

The players stand in a circle. One player runs around inside the circle and tags another player, who tries in turn to tag the first player before he gets back to his own place in the circle. Whether he succeeds or not, he is the next tagger. Both must run without bending the knees.

Sewing Up the Gaps

All but two players form a circle without joining hands. One is given a start of ten counts before the other may try to tag him. The first one runs as fast as possible between the other players, whereupon the two between whom he ran immediately join hands, thus "sewing up the gaps." The first player may run under the joined hands to save himself, or the players may release their hold and let him pass through, immediately rejoining them to prevent his pursuer from taking advantage of the gap. The pursuer must confine himself to the open spaces. The pursuer tries to tag the other player before he sews up all the gaps.

When the player succeeds in sewing up all the gaps or when he is caught, he chooses another pursuer and the former pursuer sews up the gaps.

Pies

One player is seller, another buyer, and the other players are pies. The seller gives all the pies names and sets them in a row on the shelf facing the goal, such as a post, a tree, or something the pies can encircle fairly easily. The buyer stands a fair distance from the pies with the seller near him. The buyer says, "Have you any pies for sale?" The seller says, "What kind do you want?" The buyer says, "Have you any pumpkin (any kind he chooses) pie?" If there is a pumpkin pie, he immediately starts to encircle the goal, and the buyer tries to tag him before he gets back to his seat. If he is tagged, he is set on a new shelf opposite or well separated from the original one. If he gets back to his place without being tagged, the pie becomes the buyer, the buyer sits on the new shelf, and the seller remains the same. This continues until all the pies have been disposed of or until the players choose to stop playing.

Tin

This is a game for boys. The tinman goes around among the players and says to each in turn, "How many pounds of tin do you want?" Each buys the number of pounds he wishes. The tinman goes around again, saying, "Where's the money for my tin?" and collects a forfeit from each. He then calls out any one of the players and holds a forfeit behind him saying, "How many pounds of tin behind your back?" whereupon that player guesses the name of the owner. If his guess is correct, the guesser gives the owner as many "punches" as he bought pounds of tin. If it is not correct, the owner of the forfeit runs to a goal previously agreed upon, and the guesser tries to catch him. If he catches him, the tinman throws the forfeit as far as he can, and the owner goes and gets it. If, however, he gets to the goal without being tagged, the tinman hands him the forfeit. This is repeated until all forfeits are redeemed.

Prove It

All the players line up on a goal. It says, "I give you ten (any number) of giant, scissors, baby, lady, rabbit (or other) steps," designating a different number for each kind of step. All take the steps as granted, moving directly away from the goal, after which, It calls upon one of the players to prove it in (any reasonable number) of scissors (or other) steps. To prove it, the player must cover the distance from the place where he stands to the goal in the number (no more and no less) and kind of steps assigned. If the player thinks this is unfair he says, "Prove it yourself," and *It* must do so. If *It* succeeds, he becomes a rescuer and the other player becomes *It;* but if he fails, he continues to be *It* and the other player becomes a rescuer. If, on the other hand, the player originally assigned the task of "proving it" had done so, he would have become a rescuer and *It* would have continued to be *It;* but if he had failed, he would have become *It,* and *It* would have become a rescuer.

The function of the rescuer is that of running out from the goal and bringing in other players to safety. *It* may tag a rescuer at any time he is off the goal, and thereby make that player *It* and himself a rescuer.

The players who have taken their steps at the beginning of the game and therefore are trying to get back to the goal may do so by running back when *It* is engaged with other players or by cautiously moving a few inches at a time when *It* is not looking their way. Should *It* see anyone moving, that player becomes *It.*

Prove It in Colors

This game is the same as *Prove It,* with the following exceptions: All the players walk away from the goal and continue until *It* calls "Stop," whereupon they all stop, turn about and face the goal. *It* then calls upon a player to prove it in purple rabbit steps, for example, or in any color and any kind of steps. The number of letters in the name of the color determines the number of steps to be taken. The game then proceeds the same as *Prove It.*

Fox and Geese, or Cut the Pie

This game is played in the snow. In preparation for the game, the players run in a circle and then run across, making lines like the cuts of a pie. The game is as follows: One player is the fox and the others are geese. The fox may tag a goose unless he is standing in the center at the intersection of the lines. Only one player may occupy this place at one time, and the player occupying it must give way to any other one who comes to take it. If the first player does not give way, he may be tagged by the fox. All running must be confined to the paths. A player who violates this rule becomes the fox, as does any player tagged by the fox.

Magician

The players run freely about trying to avoid being tagged by *It,* who is the "magician." When tagged, a player must stop instantly and may not move unless freed from the spell by being touched by a free player, after which he may rejoin the game and try to free other players. The aim of the magician is to render all the players inactive.

Pom Pom Pullaway

The players stand on one side of the street (or other open space). *It* stands midway between street curbs or other parallel goal lines and calls "Pom pom pullaway, come away or I'll fetch you!" When the call is finished, but not before, all must run immediately for the opposite goal, and *It* may start to tag. He tags as many as possible, and those tagged join *It* as taggers and stand midway between goals until *It* finishes the call. The game continues until all are caught. Boundaries are usually set, outside of which the players may not run.

Fish Net

The players run about freely as in tag. *It* runs and tags a player. These two join adjacent hands and both become taggers. The next player who is tagged joins hands with his tagger, and so on, until five are in line. Thereafter the taggers must encircle the player before he is considered caught. A player may dodge under the joined hands to escape, provided the other players have not yet joined hands in a circle about him. As the players are caught, they join the taggers. The game continues until all are caught.

Is It Far to Timbuktu?

The players join hands in a line, the two tallest at the head. Remaining where they are, these two join both hands and make a gate while the one at the foot leads the line around in a curve until he is standing before the gate. The following conversation takes place between the line of players and the gatekeepers:

Players: How many miles to Timbuktu?
Gatekeepers: Twenty miles.
Players: Can we get there by candlelight?
Gatekeepers: Yes and back again.
Players: Then open the gates and let us go through!

The first child leads the line through the gate; and as the last one goes under, all break and run, pursued by the gatekeepers, who catch as many as they can. Those caught drop out, and the game is repeated until all are caught. The gatekeepers choose their successors for the next round.

Bull in the Ring

The players join hands in a circle with one, the bull, in the center. The bull runs against the joined hands of the players, endeavoring to break through. He must not use his hands in doing so. As soon as he has broken through, all the players pursue him; and the one bringing him to a standstill is the bull for the repetition of the game.

Mother Carey's Chickens

I.   One player is the fox; six or seven other players line up, one behind the other, each with both arms about the waist of the one in front of him. "Mother Carey," the one at the head of the line, with arms extended, swings the line about to keep the fox from tagging the last chicken. As soon as he does so, the players line up again with new players for Mother Carey, the fox, and the last chicken.

II.   One player is tagger; the others line up, one behind the other, each with both arms about the waist of the one in front, as in I. The tagger says to the one at the head of the line, "Jacob, what do you want?" He replies, "Catch the last one if you can." The last one at the foot of the line runs and tries to get into place at the head of the line without being tagged. The line helps him by swinging about as in I. If he is tagged, he drops out of the game; if successful, he remains at the head of the line. The game proceeds until all are either tagged and out of the game or have got to the head successfully.

Fox and Chickens

The mother hen stands at one end of the field, the chickens stand behind a line at the opposite end, and the fox stands off at one side midway between them. The mother calls "Come home my chickens." They answer, "We're afraid the old fox will get us" The mother calls again emphatically "Come home!" whereupon they must immediately run for home. The fox tags as many as he can and puts them in his den, where they must remain until all the chickens are tagged. The mother goes to the opposite end of the field and calls the chickens again. The game continues until all are caught. After several chickens are caught, the fox may choose one of them as a helper, should he wish to do so.

Center Base

The players stand in a circle with one in the center, who throws a ball to any one of the players and then runs outside the circle. This player catches the ball, runs to place it in the center of the circle, and tries to tag the thrower before he can run and touch the ball. Both the thrower and the catcher must run outside the circle after throwing and placing the ball in the center respectively. The one who succeeds is next to throw the ball.

Free Tag

One player, who is *It,* tries to tag any one of the other players whenever he is not touching wood, cement, or whatever has been agreed upon as making the players safe. The player thus tagged becomes *It,* and the one who tagged him joins the other players.

Straddle Ball

One player, who is *It*, stands astride a basketball while the other players stand about and try to kick the ball from between his feet without being tagged or detected by him. He may reach out and tag a player only when the ball is between his feet, but if he succeeds, the player tagged is *It*.

When the ball is kicked successfully, the player who kicked it runs pursued by *It*, his purpose being to lead *It* in a chase and then get back and touch the ball before *It* can tag him. If he succeeds, *It* continues as *It*; if not, the other player is *It*.

Often *It* is not aware of who kicked the ball, in which case, any other player, instead of the one who kicked the ball, may deceive him by running. When *It* is thus deceived, he continues as *It* whether or not he tags the player.

Slap Tag

The players are divided into two equal groups. They stand facing each other in two lines from fifteen to twenty feet apart, with one hand extended with palm upturned. A player is chosen to start the game. He runs across to the opposite line and, moving along the line, touches the upturned palms of the players lightly. Suddenly slapping a palm vigorously, he runs for his *own place* pursued by the one whose hand he slapped. If he is caught before reaching his own place in the line, he goes to the end of the tagger's line and thereafter plays on that side. Whether he is caught or not, his pursuer repeats the play, tagging one from the opposite side. The side which has the greatest number of players at the end of the game wins.

Have You Seen My Sheep?

I.   The players stand in a circle. One runs around the outside and stands behind any player saying, "Have you seen my sheep?" That player asks, "What does he look like?" The first player describes any one of the players who, as soon as he recognizes himself as the person described, tries to tag the describer before he can run around the outside of the circle and get back to his own place in the circle. If he is tagged, he is *It* again; if not, the tagger becomes *It*.

II.   This is the same as I with the following exceptions: A player runs around and touches another on the shoulder. That player faces about, and after repeating the conversation as in I, the first player describes any one of the players in the circle. The other player tries to guess who it is. He may have three guesses, and if he succeeds, he becomes *It*, but if he fails, the first player is *It* again.

Hang Tag

One or more players are *It*. The other players are safe when hanging by their hands with their feet off the ground. Before beginning the game the players decide how many players may hang on each of the available objects. To give a dare the players run from one place to another, or they may drop to the ground to rest, and thereby risk being tagged. One player may displace another at any time.

Higher Than the Ground

One or more players are *It*. The other players are safe when they are standing on something higher than the ground. To give a dare, they run from one place to another, and one player may displace another. When a player is tagged he becomes *It*, and the one who tagged him joins the group.

Shadow Tag

This is a tag game in which the tagging consists of *It's* stepping on the shadow of a player, who is thereby made *It*. The game must be played in either sunlight or bright moonlight.

Hip

The players run freely about the play space while a tagger and his assistant try to tag them, and thereby put them out of the game. The assistant must hold a player he has caught until the tagger comes and touches him. The tagger needs only to touch those he catches. The game continues until all are out of the game.

Tag in a Circle

The players stand in a circle. One of the players runs around inside the circle, tags another player, and runs directly back to his place while the other player tries to tag him. Whether he is tagged or not, the first player goes back to his own place and the other one becomes tagger.

Jim Blows Out

With the exception of one, who is "Jim"—the tagger—the players are distributed in four corner goals in a play space sixty or more feet square. "Jim" stands in the center, and when he claps his hands all the players must run to a new goal while keeping within the boundaries. During this change of goals "Jim" tags as many as possible, and these players become taggers with him. The last one caught is "Jim" for the next round.

Pass the Pebble

All the players stand about while one goes around pretending to drop a pebble into the hands of each of the players, who hold the palms together. When he has been completely around the group and has left it in one player's hands, the one who has it slyly slips away and runs for a goal previously determined by the group, and all try to catch him. The one who succeeds passes the pebble the next time. If none succeeds, the runner passes the pebble for the next round.

Cat and Rat

The players join hands in a circle with one (the rat) in the center and another (the cat) outside. The cat tries to catch the rat by slipping under the joined hands. The players protect the rat and try to prevent the cat from catching him. When the rat is caught, both players choose others to take their roles.

Cats and Rats

The players stand with hands joined in a circle and number consecutively round the circle. Number One (the rat) goes into the circle, and Numbers Two and Three (the cats) go outside. The rat tries to run round three players in succession without being tagged by the cats. He may maneuver between each if he finds it advantageous to do so, since he may be tagged only when he is encircling a player. The rat is safe when his head is inside the circle made by the joined hands of the players; but if tagged while his head is outside, he is caught. If caught, he joins the circle, Number Two becomes the rat, Number Three remains a cat, and Number Four becomes a cat. If the rat succeeds in encircling three players, he wins but joins the circle, and the game proceeds as described until all the players have had a turn at being the rat.

Stone Witch

The players run freely about trying to avoid being tagged by *It*. The tagged players are turned to stone and must stand with arms outstretched until freed by being touched by a free player. The aim of the tagger is to get all the players turned to stone simultaneously.

Cross Tag

The players run about to escape the tagger, who, once he has started to pursue a player, must continue until another player runs between him and the player he is pursuing. When this occurs, the tagger must change his course and pursue the player who ran between him and the player he was formerly pursuing. Or, the player who ran between the tagger and the player he was pursuing becomes tagger.

Black and White Stoop Tag, or Stoop Tag

I.　　The players are scattered about the play space; and the boys and girls play against each other. The leader twirls a cardboard disk painted black on one side and white on the other. When the black side is turned toward the players, the boys try to tag the girls before they drop in a stooping position. Any who are tagged while standing erect or even partially erect are out of the game. When the white side of the disk is toward the players, the girls tag the boys. Those tagged drop out of the game.

II.   After the disk is twirled, the tagging continues for three or four minutes, the players running about giving a dare to the taggers, and as soon as any are tagged they drop out of the game. After several rounds, on a signal from the leader, all who dropped out come into the game again.

Robber

One player, who is the robber, stands in a space marked off as his den. The other players join hands in a circle and walk around singing:

It is so nice in the woods to - day, no rob-ber is hid - den a - mong the hay, When the clock strikes one, there seems to be none, But you'll see one a - live when the clock strikes five.

On the last word of the song, but not before, the circle breaks up, and the players run anywhere within the limits set for playing, to escape the robber, who tries to tag them. When a player is tagged, he immediately goes into the robber's den, where he stays during the remainder of the game. The robber continues tagging until he has tagged three players. He then returns to his den while the others form the circle again and the game continues until all are tagged. The last one tagged is robber for the repetition of the game.

I Have a Little Dog

The players stand in a circle with both hands behind them. One player runs around outside the circle, touching the hands lightly and saying, "I have a little dog, and he won't bite you, and he won't bite you," etc., until he comes to the one whom he wishes to tag, whereupon he slaps his hands and adds, "but he will bite you!" and runs for his own place in the circle pursued by the other player who tries to tag him. Whether he is caught or not, the pursuer has the next turn, and the first player returns to his own place in the circle.

Hound and Rabbits

I.   The players stand in groups of three, two joining hands to make a hollow tree with the third (a rabbit) inside. One extra player is the hound, and another the rabbit. The hound chases the rabbit, who may run into any tree thereby forcing out the other rabbit. If the hound tags the rabbit, the hound immediately becomes the rabbit and the rabbit the hound.

II.   This is played the same as I, with this exception: every time a rabbit runs into a tree, one of the players forming the tree becomes the rabbit and the rabbit becomes a part of the tree, thus giving all a chance to run.

Run Old Bear

A space is marked off for the bear's den and another for the players' goal. The bear stands with his back to the players, who come as near to him as they dare. One player, who has been chosen previously, calls "Run old bear!" whereupon the players run for home pursued by the bear, who tags as many as he can. Those tagged are put in the bear's den, and must stay there until all are caught, unless the bear should choose one of them to take his place while he rests.

Hopping and Jumping Games

General Rules for Hopscotch Games:

1. The diagram on which the play takes place is drawn on the sidewalk with chalk or scratched on the ground with a stick. The spaces vary in size but they are ample for the feet of the players as they hop from one space to another.

2. A small stone or chip of china, which the children call a "lager," thrown or kicked into the spaces must not touch a line after it lands in the space, nor may it be touched by the player's foot unless it is when he kicks it as the particular play requires. In kicking the lager out, it must go over the base line; otherwise it is a miss and puts the player out.

3. Changing from one foot to the other in hopping in any given play is a miss and puts the player out, as does putting both feet to the ground, unless the play permits it.

4. The children draw their diagrams as large or small as they choose; and, when the play becomes too easy for them, they increase the difficulties by adding more spaces, by making the spaces smaller or larger, and by using other devices that occur to them.

5. In many hopscotch games the player who completes the required play without missing may place his initials in any space he chooses. Thereafter, he may rest in that space (place both feet on the ground); but when he continues, he must hop on the foot on which he began. All players may rest in the spaces in which their initials are written but must hop over those spaces containing initials of the other players.

6. Hopscotch is usually played either by one player or by small groups of three or four players, who play in turn, although there is no limit to the number that may play.

While children usually hop on their best hopping foot, it is advisable to challenge them to hop through the game first on one foot and then on the other.

Japanese Ladder

The diagram for this game is approximately three by six feet. The first player begins at X and hops on one foot into every space and back again over the same route. If he does so without missing, he may write his initials in any space he chooses and may rest in that space

23

thereafter. Should he miss at any point in the play, he must begin at X when his turn comes again. The aim of the game is to get one's initials in the most spaces.

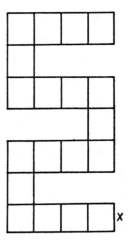

Window

I.   The diagram is approximately three by six feet. The first player starts at 1 and may rest at 8 and 21. When he makes the complete trip successfully, he may place his initials in whatever space he chooses and may rest in that space thereafter, whereas other players must hop over that space. Should he miss, he is out and when his turn comes he must begin at 1.

II.   The players, in turn, throw a stone from the base line into any square, hop into the spaces according to numerical order without touching a line, pick up the stone, and hop back over the same route. If successful, the player may write his initial in the square into which his stone fell and may rest in that space thereafter. The other players may not throw a stone into that space but must hop over it. The aim of the game is to get one's initials in the most spaces.

III.   The diagram for this game is approximately three by six feet. The first player places a flat stone, chip of china, or other small piece of suitable material, which the children call a "lager," a few inches below the base line (see diagram). Standing on one foot to begin, he hops and kicks the lager into space 1. Provided it lands in the space and does not touch a line, he hops as many times as is necessary to get in position to kick it, but must not touch it until he kicks it into space 2. He proceeds in this way to 10, when he kicks the lager out over the base line and starts over, kicking it from below the base line into space 2. Thus he begins with each space in succession and finishes with 10. When he has completed the whole series, he places his initials in any space he chooses. Thereafter, he may rest on both feet in that space. All other players must kick the lager into the space beyond this and hop over this space. Whenever a player misses, he starts with the space in which he previously failed when it is his turn to play again. The game continues until all the spaces are filled with initials.

The aim of the game is to get one's initials in the most spaces.

7	8	21
6	9	20
5	10	19
4	11	18
3	12	17
2	13	16
1	14	15

5	6
4	7
3	8
2	9
1	10

Home

Beginning at X (see diagram), the first player tries to hop on one foot into all the spaces to *Home* and back without missing. If he is successful he may write his initials in any space he chooses and may rest in that space thereafter. The other players must hop over spaces containing initials other than their own.

Should a player miss at any point in the play, he must begin at X when his turn comes again. The game continues until all the spaces are filled with initials. The aim is to get one's initials in the most spaces.

When the children draw a diagram requiring a long series of hops, they sometimes fill in two or three spaces with chalk and permit all the players to rest in them.

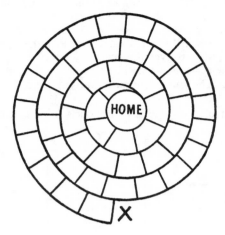

Wheel

The diagram for this game is approximately four feet in diameter. The players hop in turn from edge of the circle into 1, then into 2, from 2 to 3, and so on to 13 and out. If this is accomplished without missing, the player may place his initials in any space he chooses and rest there on repetitions of the play, while other players must hop over that space. The aim of the game is to get one's initials in the most spaces.

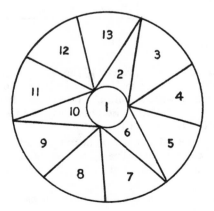

Halfway

I.   The diagram is approximately three by six feet. The first player starts at X, hops on one foot, and kicks a pebble into 1, and continues kicking it into the spaces successively as numbered until reaching the space marked "halfway" or until he misses. When he reaches "halfway" he may or may not be required to kick the pebble back, according as the players have agreed. After missing, each player begins where he left off when his turn comes again.

II.   The players *throw* the stone into 1, then hop in, and kick it out over the base line; throw it into 2, hop into 1, then into 2, and kick it out; and so on, throwing into each square consecutively. After missing, each player begins where he left off when his turn comes again.

The object of the game is to be first to complete the whole series of plays.

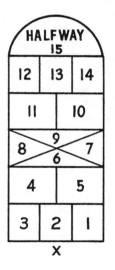

Sky Blue

The diagram is approximately seven feet long and three feet wide at the widest point.

The player stands in the space marked "start," throws his "lager" into the space marked 1, hops on one foot over 1 and lands in 2, or hops into 1 and then into 2. He then hops into 3 and lands on both feet—the left in 4 and the right in 5, hops on the foot on which he started hopping, into 6, and lands on both feet in 7 and 8. After hopping to Sky Blue, he retraces his steps until he reaches 2 or 1, as has been agreed, when he picks up his "lager" and hops out over 1 into the space marked "start," or hops into 1 and then out.

If he succeeds without missing, he places his initials in any space he chooses. Thereafter he may rest in that space, but other players must hop over it.

When all the players have had a turn at this play, the first one begins by throwing his "lager" into 2 and either hops from 1 to 3 or from 1 to 2 and continues as before. Thus the players in turn throw into spaces in numerical order and hop over the space in which the "lager" lies or hop in that space, according to agreement, until the stone has been thrown into every space.

The aim of the game is to get one's initials in the most spaces.

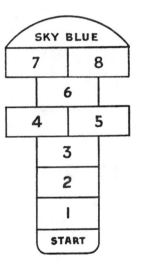

Jumping Squares

I.   A diagram is drawn on the sidewalk made up of from 16 to 48 or more squares, each a little larger than the length of the player's foot. The size of the rectangle and the number of subdivisions are usually arranged by the players with regard to their skill. Any number of children may compete in jumping squares, although it is not usual for more than three or four to play on one rectangle.

The first player stands at the base line, hops on whichever foot has been agreed upon into the squares from 1 to 48 in their numerical order, observing the general rules regarding not touching the lines, and changing from one foot to the other, although he may pause as long as he likes in any square provided he stands on his "hopping" foot. Upon reaching 48, he retraces his course, and hops from 48 to 1. Having done this without missing, he may place his initials in any square he chooses, and may rest there on both feet whenever he arrives at the square in future plays, while the other players must hop over this space. Should he miss, he must begin at 1 and hop through the whole series when his turn comes again. The players take their turns in order. The object of the game is to get one's initials in the greatest number of squares.

The game continues until all the squares are filled or until only one player is able to make the required hops.

II.　　This game is the same as I with the following exceptions: The player must hop through the series of squares first on one foot, next on the other, and then on both feet. He is entitled to place his initials in a square of his own choice when he has completed one of the three series, hopping from 1 to 28.

The game continues until all the squares are filled with initials or until only one player can make the required hops.

47	48	42	41
45	43	39	40
46	44	38	37
32	30	34	36
31	33	29	35
26	27	25	28
21	22	23	24
18	20	16	15
19	17	14	12
7	2	8	13
1	6	9	10
4	3	5	11

7	25	27	22
28	21	6	26
8	24	13	23
20	5	9	3
12	15	17	14
1	4	2	10
19	11	18	16

2	6	3	20	25	15	11
5	7	16	14	10	26	24
8	18	4	19	21	28	22
1	17	9	13	23	27	12

Jumping Rope

The play of rope jumping seems to be largely confined to girls, although boys are to be seen jumping occasionally.

I.   When the child turns her own rope, she usually repeats a learned jingle or creates one spontaneously in rhythm with her jumping, such as the following:

Down in the valley	She sang, she sang,
Where the green grass grows	She sang so sweet;
There sat (girl's name)	Along came (boy's name)
Sweet as a rose.	And kissed her cheek.

How many kisses? One, two, three, etc.

The counting continues until the jumper misses, and usually the speed is increased when the counting begins.

II.   A rope preferably three-quarters of an inch in diameter and fifteen feet long is turned by two players while the others take turns jumping as they recite jingles, often of their own spontaneous creating, such as:

1. I had a little dolly dressed in blue,
    Here are the things she used to do:
    Salute to the captain, bow to the queen,
    And turn her back on the bald-headed king.

While jumping the child salutes, bows, and turns about during the last two lines.

2. Teddy bear, Teddy bear, turn around;
    Teddy bear, Teddy bear, touch the ground;
    Teddy bear, Teddy bear, tie your shoe;
    Teddy bear, Teddy bear, now skidoo

While jumping, the child carries out in pantomime the actions suggested by the jingle, running out on "skidoo."

III.   Two ropes similar to the one used in II are turned by two players, who turn them continuously so synchronized that they are swung under the jumper's feet alternately while all the children chant a jingle, at the end of which the jumper runs out and another child runs in without a break in the rhythmic jumping. Or, a second child may run in and join the first, and later a third.

The jumpers create many feats to add difficulties when the jumping becomes too easy for them.

IV.   This is played with a fifteen-foot rope, turned by two players as in II. The players line up, one behind the other, and each in turn runs in, jumps once and runs out again. Should a player miss, she is out of the game. The break caused by a miss is momentary, the next one in line following immediately. When all have jumped once, they continue, each jumping twice, then three times, and so on, increasing the number of jumps with each round until the last one misses.

V.   This game is similar to IV with this exception: The rope is turned a few inches off the floor and is raised progressively higher until all are eliminated.

Skipping Rope

The child turns her own rope and skips (hippety-hops) over the rope on every step. Or, she may run forward and leap over the rope on every step.

Lame Fox

The lame fox stands behind a goal line. The other players come as close as they dare, and all call "Lame fox, lame fox, can't catch anybody!" whereupon they run for their goal, and the lame fox tries to tag one of them. He may have three leaps, but thereafter he must hop on one foot without touching the other to the ground. The one who is tagged either exchanges roles with the fox, or both may be taggers, and so on, each one who is tagged becoming a tagger until all are caught. While in the beginning the foxes may have three leaps, they must hop thereafter; the other players may run all the time.

Fox, Fox, Come Out of Your Den

A goal is marked off for the fox. The other players come as close as they dare and then call "Fox, fox, come out of your den!" While the fox must hop on one foot with his arms folded when tagging, the other players may run with their arms free. Should the fox unfold his arms or put both feet to the ground, the other players may beat him with their caps or hands until he reaches the goal. Provided the fox does not commit these offenses, he may tag as long as he wishes and hop back to the goal to rest and come out without a call.

All whom the fox tags become foxes and tag with him. If a fox comes out before the other players call him, they may beat him. Also if any one of the foxes puts his foot down or unfolds his arms, not only he but all the other foxes may be beaten until they reach the goal.

The game continues until all are tagged. (Belts should never be used in beating the foxes because of the danger of a child being injured by the buckle.)

Hopping Tag

I.   The players stand in a circle. One player, who is *It*, hops around, tags a player, and then hops directly back to his own place pursued by the other, who tries to tag him. Whether the tagger succeeds or not, he is *It*.

II.   The players move freely about the play space. One player, who is *It*, hops on one foot in trying to tag any one of the other players, all of whom hop wherever they choose in trying to escape him. The player who is tagged becomes *It*, and the game continues without interruption.

Jump the Shot

The players form in a circle with one in the center, who swings around the circle an old rubber or tennis shoe tied to the end of a long piece of express cord. As it slips along the floor or close to it, the players must jump to prevent being hit by it. If it touches a player's foot, he is out. This continues until all are out or until they have jumped as long as they wish.

Hopping Over Bean Bags

Bean bags are placed on the floor about a foot apart. The players take turns in trying to hop over them, one by one, first on one foot and then on the other. As their skill increases, they may hop down and back on the same foot. Or, they may hop over each bean bag, then stoop, and pick it up.

The number of bean bags used should be in relation to the ability of the players.

Jumping Hurdles

The players gallop around the room, playing they are horses, and jump over a stick held loosely as high as they can jump.

Jack Be Nimble

One player tries to jump with both feet over a block or a book a few inches high while the others say the nursery rhyme:

Jack be nimble, Jack be quick,
Jack jump over the candlestick.

Hopping Race

The whole group of players line up on a starting line, start on a signal, and hop to the goal on the left foot. Each tries to be first and not to be last. This keeps everybody in the race to the end. The leader should announce the names of the winner and of the last one to reach the goal. The players line up again and hop back to the starting line on the right foot.

Master of the Ring

A circle three or four feet in diameter is drawn on the floor, within which two players, with arms folded, try to push each other out of the ring while hopping on one foot.

Rooster Fight

Two players, with arms folded, hop on one foot, each trying to make the other put his other foot to the floor.

Hop O' My Hat

This is a game played by boys. The players place in a row seven caps, representing the days of the week. They take turns in performing each of the following feats: Hop over all the caps in turn on the right foot and back on the left; hop around each cap first on the right foot and then on the left; stand on one foot with both hands touching the ground, pick up each cap in turn, in the teeth and throw it backward over the head.

Throughout this process any boy who fails in any feat is put "through the mill;" that is, the boys line up with their feet astride, forming a tunnel through which the offender crawls head first, and, as he passes along, each boy gives him a spank or swat.

Jumping over the Brook

Parallel lines are drawn on the floor at intervals around the room to represent brooks. The players run around the room one behind the other, and try to jump over the brooks. If they fail, their "feet are wet," and therefore, they must drop out of the game.

Throwing and Catching Games

Who's Got the Ball?

The players stand scattered about in a group. *It* stands a little distance away with his back toward them. He throws a ball backward over his head, and the others try to catch it. The one who catches it, quickly hides it behind him, and the others try to deceive *It* by putting their hands behind them also. All then call "Who's got the ball?" whereupon *It* turns about and names the player he thinks has it. If correct, he has another turn at throwing; if not, the one who has the ball becomes *It*. The players may move to catch the ball but must not move after catching it or pass it to another player.

Center Catch

The players sit or stand in a circle with one player in the center, who tries to tag the ball as it is rolled from one player to another across the circle. Also, he may tag it while it is in the hands of a player. The one who is at fault in letting him do so exchanges with him.

Captain Ball

The description of this game here given is for twenty players, but as few as six and more than twenty may play.

For twenty players, the play space should be at least fifty feet long and thirty feet wide. It should be divided into two equal fields. Near each corner of the fields a circle approximately three feet in diameter and in the center, one somewhat larger is drawn. The captains occupy the center circles and the basemen those at the corners of the fields.

In the diagram, the players on one side are designated by *A, a, a'*, and those on the other side by *B, b, b'*. The guards *a'* are assigned to *b* baseman, and guards *b'* to *a* basemen (see diagram).

The captains are selected, and then they choose the other players alternately. To start the game, the two guards of the central bases stand on the central dividing line; the ball is thrown up between them and each tries to strike it into his own field so that his baseman (not the captain) can get it.

Basemen may not step outside their circles. Guards may not step inside the circles. A player may not walk or run while he holds the ball. Guards may move about freely in trying to get the ball, but they must not step over the dividing line. Any infringement of these rules constitutes a foul, and a foul by one side gives the ball to a baseman of the other side.

The object of the game is for the basemen to throw the ball to the captain, who, if he catches it, scores one point for his team. Only basemen of his team may throw the ball to the captain. The *a'* guards, therefore, try to get the ball and throw it to the *a* basemen, and the *b'* guards to *b* basemen.

One point is scored also when the ball makes a complete circuit of the bases regardless of where it starts.

The score constituting the game is determined by the players.

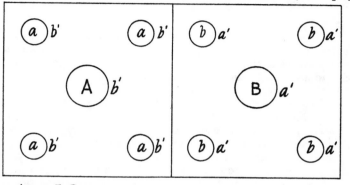

Ante-Ante-I-Over

The players are divided into two teams—*A* and *B*. The *A* team stands on one side of a summerhouse or cottage, and the *B* team on the other side. Calling "Ante-ante-i-over," an *A* player throws the ball over the house. If a *B* player catches it on the fly, his side all run around the house, either together or some one way and some the other. The *A* team also run to the opposite side of the house, but since they do not know who has the ball they may be running toward instead of away from the player who has it. The player who holds the ball touches as many of the opponents as possible with it. A player may be tagged at any time before he is past a line that is even with the far side of the house toward which he is going. Those tagged join the tagger's side.

However, if the ball is not caught by a member of the *B* team, a *B* player throws it back over the house without calling "Ante-ante-i-over; and the game proceeds as described.

Keep Ball

The players are divided into two teams, *A* and *B*. The play space is divided into four equal parts, and the players are divided into four equal groups and placed as follows:

$$| A | B | A | B |$$

A ball is tossed up between two players, one from each team, who stand on opposite sides of the middle line. Each faces his own group and tries to strike the ball toward his own players. The team that gets the ball tries to keep it. For instance, if the A's get it, they throw it over the heads of the B's to the other section of their own team, and continue throwing back and forth, scoring one point every time the ball is thrown and caught by players of the A team. The B's try to intercept the ball and to keep it by throwing it back and forth between the two sections of their team.

The players determine either upon a set time for playing or play for a set score.

Keep Away

The players are divided into two teams and wear arm bands of contrasting colors. In beginning the game, they form in couples, one from each team, and play against each other. Although it is not possible to keep these couples together, it does help to organize their play in the beginning.

Each player tries to catch the ball and to prevent an opponent from getting it. The ball is put in play by a third player's tossing it up between two others. A team scores one point every time one of its players catches the ball from a member of his own team. The players must not run with the ball or trip or indulge in any rough treatment of each other. If there is a dispute as to who has a right to the ball, it is tossed up between two players. The game requires a timekeeper for each team.

Teacher, or Go Last

I.   The players stand in a straight line. One player, who is called "teacher," stands ten or fifteen feet in front of the line of players and tosses a ball to each in turn, and each tosses it back to the teacher. Any player who fails to catch it, throws it from his place in the line to the teacher and goes to the foot of the line. If the teacher fails to catch successfully, he goes to the foot of the line; and the player at the head of the line becomes teacher. The new teacher begins where the other left off and not at the head of the line.

Older and more skilful players may use only the right or left hand in throwing and catching.

II.   The players choose sides, and the two teams compete. The teams line up and start on a signal. The teacher throws to each player in turn, and each throws to the teacher; but in case either fails to catch successfully, instead of going last in the line, they continue to throw to each other until each has caught successfully once. The teacher then throws to the next one and continues until he has thrown to every player in the line. The head player runs and stands beside the teacher ready to take the ball when the teacher receives it from the last player. The first teacher then goes to the foot of the line, the new teacher begins at the head and throws to each in turn. The game continues until every player has been teacher, and finishes when the last teacher receives the ball from the last player in the line. The team that finishes first wins the game.

Teacher on the Steps

The players sit on the bottom step of a flight of stairs. One player, who is called teacher, stands ten or fifteen feet in front of them and tosses a ball to each in turn. When a player catches successfully, he moves up one step; but when he fails, he moves down one step. If he misses when on the bottom step, he must either kneel or remain seated on that step, as previously agreed by the group. The one who first makes the trip to the top becomes the teacher, and the game proceeds, the new teacher beginning where the former one left off.

Call Ball

The players number consecutively in a circle. One goes in the center and throws the ball directly upward, calling a number *as the ball leaves his hand*. The player having this number runs to the center and tries to catch the ball before it touches the ground. If successful, he throws the ball up in the center; if not, the first player continues until someone catches successfully.

Roll Over and Back

The players sit on the floor in a circle with one in the center, who rolls the ball to each of the players in turn, and each rolls it back to him.

Wander Ball

I.   The players stand in a circle about six feet apart and throw volley-ball or basketball (any ball may be used) from one to the other while one in the center tries to touch the ball. He may do so at any time. The one who is at fault in letting him touch the ball exchanges places with him. A player may throw to either his right-hand or left-hand neighbor but must not throw the ball to any other player. A violation of this rule compels him to exchange places with the center player.

II.   This is the same as I, with the exception that the ball may be thrown across the circle or to any player. Should the ball get out of bounds or fall to the floor, any player may try to get it and put it in play before the center player can touch it. The player who is at fault when the center player succeeds in touching it exchanges places with him.

Hot Potato

The players sit or stand in a circle with one in the center, and throw a knotted towel across from one to the other, trying to prevent the center player from touching it. He may touch it at any time, even when it is in the hands of a player or when it falls outside of the circle, where it may be recovered by any of the players. The one who is at fault in letting the center player touch it exchanges places with him.

Circle Ball

The players are divided into two teams—*A* and *B*. Half of each team are guards; the other half basemen. The field is divided into two equal areas, in each of which circles, two or three feet in diameter, are drawn for as many basemen as there are on a side. Each baseman is guarded by a guard from the opponents' team. Basemen may step out of the circle with one foot, but the other must always be anchored in the circle. Guards may never step inside the circle. Should this rule be violated, the ball is given to the baseman immediately contesting.

A point is made whenever a baseman catches the ball thrown to him by another baseman on his team. Guards try to intercept the ball and throw it to basemen on their own team. Guards may not run or walk with the ball.

To begin the game, the ball is thrown up between two guards, each of whom tries to bat it into his field.

Wall Baseball

One player, the batter, stands ten or fifteen feet from the wall and throws a small hard rubber ball in the crack where a wall and pavement meet. The other players, who stand about back of him, try to catch it on the rebound. If anyone catches it, the batter is out. If no one catches it, the batter scores one point and continues throwing until the ball is caught. When it is caught, the catcher becomes batter. The players determine the number of points that constitute the game.

Throwing at a Mark Games

Blackboard Baseball

Any number of players is divided into two baseball teams. They determine upon places for first, second, and third bases, which may be three chairs placed in a row. A throwing line, corresponding to home plate, is drawn some distance from a blackboard. The distance may be in accordance with the skill of the players.

A diagram approximately two and a half feet square is drawn on the blackboard and divided into sixteen equal squares (see diagram).

Fly Caught	Home Run	Base Runner hit with fly ball
3rd Base	Strike Out	2nd Base
Four Balls	1st Base	3rd Strike caught by catcher

Various *Baseball* plays are written in the squares, and an advantageous play such as "home-run" is written near "fly caught." An eraser filled with chalk dust is used to dust over the whole square.

The teams each choose a player, who throws a tennis ball for a certain square, and the first turn to play goes to the team whose thrower hits nearest to the center of that square. The players in each team are numbered and throw as they would bat in *Baseball*.

The first player stands on the line (home plate) and throws. If the ball hits so that the impression made by it is within the lines, he scores accordingly. For instance, if it is "fly caught" he is out, and the next player throws. If he hits a line, he scores according to the space in which the ball makes the greatest impression. He has three throws, similar to three strikes in *Baseball*. As in *Baseball*, when there are three out, the other team throws.

The runs are scored as in *Baseball*. If the first player should hit

39

"second base," he goes and sits on the chair previously determined as second base. If the next player should hit the same square, he takes second base, which forces the first player to third base. If the next player hits "home-run," their team scores three runs. However, if he had hit "third base," it would have forced the men on second and third home and would have scored only two runs, leaving him on third base.

The plays as shown in the diagram are only suggestive and may be changed, although not all baseball plays can be used.

Dodge Ball

I.   The players stand in a circle with five or more in the center. The circle players try to hit those in the center with a basketball, volleyball or indoor baseball. Without a pause in the game the player who is hit exchanges places with the one who hit him. To finish the game, the players who are hit join the circle until the last one is out.

II.   The players are divided into two equal teams. The players of one team are dodgers, and play inside a circle made up of the other team, who are throwers. The dodgers are eliminated as soon as they are hit. When all have been eliminated, the teams exchange roles. The team that eliminates the other in the briefest time wins.

Battle Ball

The players are divided into two teams, and the room is divided into two equal fields. Both teams set up an equal number of Indian clubs in a row about three feet from their respective back walls, the clubs being about the same distance apart and in relatively the same position for both teams.

The players of each team are scattered about on their own side of the dividing line. An indoor or other ball is tossed up between two players in starting. The aim of the game is to knock down the opponents' clubs. A club once down is removed, as is a club accidentally knocked down by the players. If there are many players, it may be necessary to limit the distance within which they may guard the clubs. In any case they must not stand closer than three feet. The team which knocks down all the opponents' clubs first wins the game.

War Target

The diagram, which is approximately four feet long, is usually drawn on the sidewalk, but it may be smaller and be drawn on a table or board (see diagram). There may be any number of spaces for soldiers, and war may be any number desired by the players.

In the following descriptions, the players are designated as *A* and *B*.

Spaces 1 to 5 belong to *A*; and those from 11 to 15 belong to *B*. Each tries to be first to fill all his spaces with soldiers, which requires the following number of strokes: head, 1; eyes, 2; nose 1; mouth, 1; arms, 2; and legs, 2; and to equip every soldier with ten guns.

These strokes are secured by snapping a small stone or chip of china from the spot designated in the diagram, into any of the fifteen spaces. If the chip falls within the space (not touching a line), it gives the player one stroke toward making the soldier in that space. For instance, if the chip is thrown by A and falls in space 8, it may be used by A in space 3; or if thrown by B and falls in space 8, he may use it in space 13. If it falls within the space marked "war," it gives the player 20 strokes, which may be used in any space. If it falls within a space where a soldier is being drawn, it gives the player one stroke in completing that soldier, provided it does not touch a boundary line. If the soldier in that space is complete, the player may not use the stroke in another space.

The players take turns, and each continues until his chip fails to fall with a space. The one who first fills all his spaces with soldiers equipped with guns wins the game.

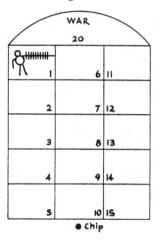

● Chip

Circle Stride

I. All the players stand in a circle with their feet astride and touching those of his neighbor on either side. One player has a basketball or volleyball, which he puts into play by trying to throw it between the feet of another player. If he succeeds, that player drops out, and the circle closes the gap. When the ball is not in play, the players' hands must be on their knees.

II. One player in the center tries to throw the ball between the feet of any one of the other players. If he is successful, he exchanges places with the victim.

Horseshoe Pitching

The equipment required for the game consists of two horseshoes for each of the players and two iron stakes, three feet long and one inch in diameter. Commercially made shoes are painted in contrasting colors and weigh two and one-half pounds.

The stakes are driven in the ground forty feet apart leaving eight inches above the ground. The distance between stakes is often shortened and lighter-weight shoes used, especially for boys.

The scoring is as follows: Each player pitches two shoes in succession. One or two shoes lying closest to or leaning against the stake and thrown by the same player score one point each. A ringer scores three points, and a double ringer thrown by the same player scores six points. When a ringer is thrown over a ringer by an opponent, neither scores. When one player throws two ringers, and an opponent throws one, the player who threw the two ringers scores three points. In case of ties no score is made by any player.

A shoe, moved from its original position by one thrown by any player, scores according to its new position. A shoe scores as a ringer only when the open ends are far enough beyond the stake so that a measuring stick applied to the ends of the shoe do not touch the stake. Fifty points constitute the game.

In starting the game, each player pitches two shoes in succession for the same stake, and the loser pitches first on the next round.

Bowling

This is a simple form of bowling, which may be played with Indian clubs or any suitable substitute and with a hockey ball or a hard baseball. The clubs are set up at one end of a long room or outdoor space about five or six inches apart (see diagram), and the players choose sides and bowl alternately from a distance of thirty or more feet. The players have one throw each and score one point for every club that falls.

Number Target

The players choose sides and stand or sit in a line. The teams take turns alternately in throwing a tennis ball or other soft ball at a target from a distance of approximately fifteen feet.

A satisfactory target is a two-foot square subdivided in sixteen equal squares and numbered from one to sixteen. The whole surface should be dusted over with a chalk-filled eraser. The thrower's score corresponds to the number of the square in which the ball makes the greatest imprint. Although there may not be an equal number of players, both teams should have an equal number of throws, and the team that has the highest score wins.

Five Back

Five tenpins or Indian clubs are set in a line so close together as barely to let a hockey ball roll between them. The kingpin is the one on the left. The players throw from a line from twenty to thirty feet from and parallel with the pins, and each gets three throws.

If all the pins go down on one throw, it is a strike and scores five. The pins are set up again, and the thrower gets his two other throws. If all the pins go down on two throws, it is a spare and the thrower gets one more throw. Nothing scores unless the kingpin goes down, but if another pin goes down on the first throw, the thrower scores two—one for each pin—even though the kingpin goes down after the other one.

Duck on a Rock

Each of the players gets a missile—a piece of brick or a rock about the size of his fist—called a duck. A stump or large rock is selected; and the players line up on a goal about fifteen or twenty feet from the rock and throw in turn, each trying to get his duck nearest to the rock. The one whose duck is farthest away is *It,* and puts his duck on the rock. The others get their ducks and again line up. Without regard to turns, they throw their ducks trying to knock *It's* duck off the rock. After having thrown, the player goes out and stands near his duck, being careful not to get hit. He may seize his duck and run for goal at any time, but he may be tagged by *It* provided *It's* duck is on the rock. If *It* succeeds in tagging anyone, *It* runs to the rock; and if he can tap his duck on the rock three times before the player he tagged can get his duck on the rock and tag him, he may go home safely; that is, he may not be tagged while going to the goal. In any case, the new *It* places his duck on the rock as quickly as possible and begins tagging. During this exchange of roles is a good time for the players to get back to goal.

While the tagging is in progress, the other players try to save the one who is being pursued, by knocking *It's* duck off the rock. They should be alert in observing whether *It's* duck is still on the rock at the instant he tags a player.

Even though he may not have picked up his duck, a player may be tagged any time after he has touched it with his hand, although he may stand with his foot on it as long as he likes while he waits for a favorable moment to snatch it and run for goal.

Whenever *It* thinks any player's duck is within a hand span of the rock, he may challenge the owner and himself try to span the distance. If he can do so, the owner becomes *It*.

Stop

The players are numbered consecutively and stand in a circle. One player goes into the center, throws up a ball, and calls a number as the ball leaves his hand. The player having this number tries to catch the ball before it touches the ground.

When the number is called, all, with the exception of the one having this number, including the thrower, run away from the circle and continue running until the player whose number was called catches the ball and calls "Stop!" whereupon all remain motionless. The catcher may not take a step after he catches the ball but, standing where he caught it, rolls it at the feet of any player he chooses. If he hits anyone or if a player toward whom he rolls it moves his foot, he is out. When a player is not hit, the circle is formed again; and the previous thrower starts the game by throwing the ball up in the center and calling another number. When a player is hit, he throws the ball up in the center; and when it is caught, he drops out of the game. This continues until all the players are out.

Guard the Gate

The players sit on the floor in a circle an arm's length apart. Each guards the space on his own right. A volleyball (or other ball) is vigorously rolled by the players in the effort to get it through the open spaces. Anyone who lets the ball go through the space on his right drops out of the game.

When unskilful players under seven or eight years of age are playing, it is best to have them continue in the game, keeping count of all who guard their gates successfully.

Shooting Gallery

The players choose sides, and the two teams line up, facing each other fifteen or twenty feet apart. The players of one team place their feet as they like and hold the position as nearly immovable as possible while each of the players of the other team rolls the ball in turn at the feet of the players of that team. A player whose foot is touched by the ball or who moves his foot as the ball approaches him, is eliminated. If the foot of more than one player is hit by the ball, these players are out.

The throwing continues until all are out. A record of the number of throws required to put the team out is kept. When the last player is eliminated, the teams reassemble, and those who formerly were targets become throwers while the former throwers line up as targets.

Bunny in the Hole

I.   This is a game for boys. The players place their caps (or dig shallow holes) close to a fence or wall, one beside the other. One boy volunteers to be *It*. The others stand in a line parallel with, and about fifteen feet from, the caps, or each may stand near his own cap. *It* rolls the ball from the line, endeavoring to get it into a cap, and continues until he succeeds, whereupon the owner immediately gets the ball and throws it at the fleeing players, who run as far as they can. The thrower may run a few feet but must not actually pursue the players. If he hits a player, that player gets one demerit a (pebble in his cap) and becomes *It*. If he fails to hit a player, the thrower gets a demerit and becomes *It*. When any player gets three demerits, he is "put through the mill" by all who have no demerits. Putting him through the mill may be done in one of two ways: either the boys stand in a row with feet astride while the victim crawls down the "tunnel" and gets a "swat" from each boy as he goes through or the victim stands facing the wall with his hand flat against it while the players who have no demerits get three throws with the ball at his hand with their eyes open and three with them shut.

II.   This is played the same as I with the following exceptions: The one into whose cap the ball rolls, runs, pursued by *It*, who gets the ball and tries either to tag him with it while he holds it in his hand or to throw it and hit him with it before he gets back to his cap. If *It* succeeds in tagging the other player, that player gets a demerit and becomes *It*, but if not; *It* gets a demerit and continues as *It*.

Bird Hunter

One player is hunter, and the others are birds. The hunter throws a ball at the birds, who may run freely about within boundaries determined by the players. When the birds are hit with the ball, they become dogs and help the hunter by recovering and throwing the ball to him. The hunter is the only one who may hit the birds. The last bird to be hit becomes the hunter for a repetition of the game.

Center Dodge

The players sit or stand in a circle with one player in the center. Those forming the circle roll a ball, trying to hit the feet of the center player, who may run about and dodge as he chooses. He changes places with the player who succeeds in hitting him.

This may be played with two or more players in the center. When there are several players in the center, they may be eliminated one by one to finish the game.

Center Club Bowl

The players are divided into two teams and stand in a circle. They take turns in trying to bowl down three Indian clubs set in triangular

formation about ten inches apart in the center of the circle. Each
scores for his team the number of clubs he knocks down. Both teams
have the same number of turns, and the one having the highest score
wins.

Bean Bag Board

The board on which this game is played should be about two
and a half feet long and one and a half wide. Two holes, one approximately three inches in diameter and the other four and a half inches,
should be cut in triangular formation ten or more inches apart.

The game consists in throwing bean bags from a throwing line,
the distance being determined by the ability of the players. The number
of points constituting the game may be as agreed by the players. A
successful throw through the smaller holes scores two points each and
through the large hole one point.

Bowl out of a Circle*

The players stand in a circle. A chalk circle about eighteen inches
in diameter is drawn on the floor, and five or six marbles or balls are
placed on crosses within the circle. The players take turns in trying
to bowl these out of the circle with a ball or large marble.

Bowl into a Circle*

The players stand in a circle. A chalk circle is drawn on the floor,
and the players take turns in trying to roll a ball so that it will stop
within the circle.

One, Two, Three, Roll*

The players sit or stand in a circle. Five or six players are given
tennis balls, each marked with a different color. All say, "One, two,
three, roll," whereupon each rolls his ball endeavoring to make it
stop within a circle about eighteen inches in diameter drawn on the
floor.

Throw into a Box*

The players stand in a circle and take turns in trying to throw a
ball or bean bag into a box in the center of the circle. Each has three
turns in succession.

---

*These games may be played by two teams by numbering the
players 1, 2; 1, 2; etc., round the circle and having the 1's play
against the 2's. They may play alternately; or, in games in which
a ball is rolled at a target in the center, the player nearest whom the
ball rolls may be the next to roll it, thus adding to the interest.
However, the players should all have a turn eventually, and none
should have more turns than another.

Don't Hit

The players stand in a circle. Three Indian clubs or other objects are placed in the center in triangular formation about ten inches apart. The players take turns in trying to roll a ball between any two of them and to avoid hitting them.

Throwing Cards

The players are divided into two teams, and stand in a circle. A deck of playing cards is distributed among the players of one team, and another deck of contrasting color or design is distributed among the players of the other team. On a signal, all throw their cards endeavoring to make them fall into a box (or wastebasket) placed in the center of the circle. The team getting the greatest number in the box wins.

Concentric Circles Target

A target of concentric circles may be drawn on the floor (or on a board or table), and the spaces numbered. The players take turns in tossing a beanbag or in snapping a checker into the spaces, and score according to the space in which it falls clear of the line.

Bouncing Ball Games

O'Leary

This game, which seems to be played exclusively by girls, consists in batting a small rubber ball with the palm of the right hand while performing a set of prescribed movements and chanting various jingles, the first of which is as follows:

One, two, three, O' Lear - y, four, five, six, O' Lear - y Seven, eight,

Optional Ending

nine, O' Lear - y ten O' Lear - y Post-man. ten O' Lear - y of U. S. A.

After a miss the player must, on her next turn, begin with the exercise on which she missed.

The movements are as follows:

1. The ball is bounced with the right open palm three times while the player chants "One, two, three." On "O" she bats the ball more forcefully, making it rebound higher, and as she says "Leary" swings the right leg from left to the right over the ball on the rebound. The whole movement is repeated while the second line of the jingle is chanted and again on the third line. On the last line the player bounces the ball on "post" and catches and holds it on "man," ready to begin the second movement, or she may bounce it on "post" and again on "man" and then catch it.

The whole first movement is repeated and the following movements are substituted for the swinging of the right leg over the ball:

2. The left leg is swung from right to left over the ball.
3. The right leg is swung from right to left over the ball.
4. The left leg is swung from left to right over the ball.
5. The player catches the bottom edge of her skirt with the left hand, sometimes twisting it a bit, and as she chants "O'Leary" and bats the ball she swings her left arm forward so that the ball drops downward through the opening between her left arm and skirt.
6. This is the same as 5 with the exception that the ball rebounds upward through the opening on "O'Leary."
7. The player takes her weight on her left foot, keeping it immovable

48

while she touches her right heel forward on "one," then the toe backward on "two," and the heel forward again on "three," and so on, keeping the movement in perfect and continuous rhythm throughout the verse.

8. This is a repetition of 7 with the left foot in action.

9. The chant for this movement is as follows:

> Kewpie, Kewpie, shine my shoes;
> Kewpie, Kewpie, shine my shoes;
> Kewpie, Kewpie, shine my shoes;
> So early in the morning.

The ball is batted continuously while the right foot is moved back and forth across in front of the left, which must be kept immovable, the right toe touching the floor first to the left and then to the right.

10. Player repeats the heel-toe movement with right foot, as in 7, on "one, two, three" and swings the right leg to the right over the ball on "O'Leary."

11. This is a repetition of 10 with the left foot in action.

12. The player repeats the heel-toe movement, as in 7, and holds the skirt as in 5. She bounces the ball on "one, two" swings the right leg over the ball on "three," lets the ball fall through the opening between her left arm and skirt on "O'Leary," and catches the ball on the rebound.

13. The chant for this movement is as follows:

> Jack, Jack, pump the water;
> Jack, Jack, pump the water;
> Jack, Jack, pump the water;
> So early in the morning.

The player bounces the ball on "Jack, Jack," bats it with great force on "pump," so that it bounces higher than her head, and turns completely to the right about (clockwise) in time to bat it again on beginning the second line of the chant. She repeats the same movements on the third line, and on the fourth bounces the ball three times, catching it on the fourth count.

14. The chant for this movement is as follows:

> Jack, Jack, shoot the skyrocket;
> Jack, Jack, shoot the skyrocket;
> Jack, Jack, shoot the skyrocket;
> So early in the morning.

The player bounces the ball as in 1 on "Jack, Jack," strikes it upward with the open palm on "shoot" and turns completely to the right about in time to repeat the same on the second line of the chant. She repeats the same on the third line, and on the fourth line bounces the ball three times and catches it on the fourth count.

15. The chant for this movement is as follows:

Jack, Jack, open the gate;
Jack, Jack, open the gate;
Jack, Jack, open the gate;
So early in the morning.

The player bounces the ball three times as in 1, the left hand holding the right wrist, and lets the ball come up, through the opening between her arms, from below on "open the gate"; she repeats this on the second and third lines and bounces and catches the ball as in 14, on the last line.

16. The chant is the same as 15 with the exception that "let me in" is substituted for "open the gate." The movement is also the same with the exception that the ball falls downward between the arms.

17. This is the same as 1 with the exception that the right leg is swung over the ball twice on "O'Leary, O'Leary." The chant runs:

One, two, three, O'Leary, O'Leary,
Four, five, six, O'Leary, O'Leary,
Seven, eight, nine, O'Leary, O'Leary,
Ten, O'Leary, O'Leary, postman.

18. This is a repetition of 17 with the left leg swung over the ball.

19. This is a repetition of 6 with the exception that the ball bounces through the opening twice in quick succession.

20. This is a repetition of 1 with the exception that the right leg is swung to the right over the ball on every bounce.

21. This is a repetition of 20 with the left leg in action.

22. This is the same as 5 with the exception that the ball passes through the opening made by the left arm and the skirt on every bounce.

Bounce Over and Back

One player stands in the center of the circle and bounces the ball to each of the other players in turn, and each bounces it back to him. There is no penalty for failing to catch it. The game may be varied according to the skill of the players by catching with the right or left hands or both.

Multiplication Table

Although any number of players may play this game, it is best to confine it to two. It is often played by one.

A circle approximately three feet in diameter, divided by six or more lines radiating from the center, is drawn on the sidewalk. Any number may be drawn in the center and in the spaces between the lines (see diagram). The player walks around the circle, bouncing a ball into one space after another and announcing the product of the center number multiplied by the number of the space in which the ball strikes. The players compete in trying to make the complete circuit without making a mistake. The ball must strike the space and not a line; it must be caught on the first bounce; and the product must be announced within the time agreed upon. In case of failure, the player must begin at the beginning and complete the circuit without a mistake. The one who does so first wins the game. The numbers are changed by the players to suit the particular playing group.

While the size of the diagrams is determined by the players, the spaces should be large enough to permit the player to bounce the ball easily without touching the lines with the ball or the foot.

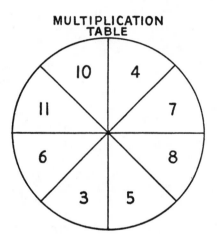

MULTIPLICATION
TABLE

Wall Ball

The players number off and stand scattered about. One player throws a ball against a wall and calls a number as the ball leaves his hand. The player whose number was called must catch it on the first bounce. If he is successful, he throws; if not, the first thrower throws again. Or, the players stand about while one of them throws a ball against a wall. Whoever catches it either on the first bounce or on the fly, as has been agreed, is next to throw it.

Call Ball

The players stand in a circle and number consecutively. One stands in the center and throws a ball directly upward. *As it leaves his hand,* he calls a number. The player whose number is called must catch the ball on the first bounce. If successful, he stays in the center and throws up the ball; if not, the first player throws again and continues until someone succeeds in catching it.

Roly Poly

I.   A rectangle approximately eight by three feet is drawn on the sidewalk, and subdivided into from six to twelve equal spaces (see diagram). The children then write names of familiar objects in the spaces. The game is usually played by not more than three or four children, although any number may play. One child may play alone.

The first player stands in front of the base line, rolls a rubber ball into the space marked "girls" and, stepping with only one foot into that space, tries to pick up the ball before it rolls out of the space or touches a line. Should either the ball or the player's foot touch a line at any time or should he stand on both feet, he is out, and the next player has a turn. However, if he catches the ball within the space, he stands on one foot, bounces the ball in the space marked "girls" and continues to bounce it while reciting girls' names in succession, one on every bounce as he steps in one space after another.

Upon reaching "teachers" he steps out and rolls the ball into the space marked "boys" and repeats the whole performance. Thus the player rolls the ball into the spaces in succession and proceeds as described.

As the ball is rolled into successive spaces, the player must run from the first one to the one in which the ball is rolled, stepping one foot in each, and catch the ball before it rolls out. This is a difficult feat, since he must not touch a line with his foot.

Having completed the series without a mistake, the player reverses his course, begins at "teachers," and repeats the whole series of plays. Should he miss in any space, he begins in that space when his turn comes again.

When a player has completed all these plays, he may write his initials in any space he chooses and may rest there on both feet when he comes to that space again. Also he is not required to roll the ball into it subsequently, nor name the class of objects as indicated in that space. The other players, however, must roll the ball into that space, recover the ball without stepping into it, bounce the ball in it, step over that space, and proceed as before.

Unless so stipulated, it is not obligatory for a player to recite names different from those used by other players, but each player must recite different names as he moves from space to space.

The players continue in turn until all the spaces are filled with initials. When a player misses he begins in the space in which he failed when his turn comes again. The aim is to get one's initials in the most spaces.

II.   The player stands at the base line and rolls, catches and bounces the ball saying "girls" on the first bounce as in I, then steps into the next space and bounces the ball saying a girl's name, such as, Martha. He proceeds from one space to the next, spelling M-a-r-t-h-a and bouncing the ball once in each space for each of the letters. When reaching the last space he retraverses the route (but bounces the ball only once in the last space) and continues until the last letter of the name occurs, when he bounces the ball in the last space, in this case the one marked "teachers." He may then place his initials in any space he chooses and may rest on both feet in that space thereafter.

III.   This version is played the same as I, with the following exceptions: After completing the series from "girls" to "teachers" and from "teachers" to "girls," the player recites the following, bouncing the ball, as before, in successive spaces, once on every word: "My mother told me to put my name in this box. M-a-r-y, b-o-x." He then writes his initials in any space he chooses, and thereafter is not required to roll the ball into that space.

IV.   This version is played the same as I with the following additions: After having completed the series of plays as described in I, the player starts with "girls," bounces the ball in each space, saying "girls," "boys," "colors," and so on. Having reached "teachers," he retraces his course but names only one of each class, as "Miss Smith," "gum drops," and "overcoat," After he finishes this series, he goes through letters of the alphabet, follows that by spelling out his own name in full, and writes his initials in the space in which the last letter of his name occurs.

Cars	Animals
Flowers	Toys
Fruits	Vegetables
Colors	Clothing
Boys	Candy
Girls	Teachers

Bounce Up Flies

The players are scattered about the field. One player, who stands separated from and facing them, bounces a ball into their midst. The one who catches it on the first bounce is next to bounce it. If no one catches it, the first player bounces it again and continues until someone catches it.

Bounce into a Box

The players stand in a circle, and each has a turn at bouncing a soft rubber ball and trying to make it land in a box placed in the center of the circle. Each player takes three turns in succession.

Ball Drill

The players are all equipped with rubber balls, and one of them leads the others in bouncing, tossing, and dribbling the ball to various rhythms played by a pianist. Or, the players may create their own plays in their own way.

Jackstones

The game of Jackstones is popular with little girls but it is quite skilful enough for more pretentious players. It is usually played on a floor or doorstep with a golf ball or small rubber ball, and with from six to twelve small six pronged steel pieces called jackstones.

The jackstones are gathered up in the right hand and thrown upon the floor so that they are separated. This the children call "throwing scatters." It is best not to have the jackstones more than two or three inches apart. If they fall so that two are entangled, one must be taken away without moving the other one, and this must be done while a play is in progress.

The ball is always tossed up with the right hand, the jackstones are always caught with the right hand, and the ball is caught with the right hand after it has bounced once, unless otherwise indicated.

The rules of the game are as follows: The players take turns alternately, and each plays until she misses. The misses are: failure to complete the whole play without a mistake; striking a jackstone with the ball as it bounces; and moving one jackstone while picking up another. When a player misses, the turn passes to another player, and when the first player's turn comes again, the play in which the miss occurred must be made from the beginning.

The player must always pick up the required number of jackstones first, and take the remaining ones later. For instance, if six jackstones are being used, and the play requires that they be picked up four at a time, the four must be taken first, and then the two.

Any combination of plays may be determined by the players. In fact, children develop new and more difficult plays as they develop skill. Six jackstones are used in the following plays:

1. Babies: Throw scatters, toss up the ball with the right hand, pick up a jackstone with the right hand, transfer it to the left hand, and catch the ball after it has bounced once. Continue this play, picking up one jackstone at a time until all are picked up. Throw scatters again, and pick up the jackstones two at a time; throw scatters, and pick up three at a time; throw scatters, and pick up four, and then two; throw scatters, and pick up five, and then one; and throw scatters, and pick up six at a time.

2. Upcast: Throw scatters, toss up the ball, pick up a jackstone, catch the ball, toss up the ball, transfer the jackstone to the left hand, and catch the ball after it has bounced once. Proceed as in 1.

3. Downcast: Throw scatters, toss up the ball, pick up a jackstone, catch the ball, drop the ball, transfer the jackstone to the left hand, and catch the ball after it has bounced once. Proceed as in 1.

4. Double upcast: Throw scatters, toss up the ball, pick up a jackstone, and catch the ball. Toss up the ball, transfer the jackstone to the left hand, pick up another jackstone, and catch the ball after it bounces once. Afer picking up the last jackstone touch the floor instead of picking up the jackstone in finishing the play. Proceed as in 1.

5. Double downcast: Throw scatters, toss up the ball, pick up a jackstone, and catch the ball. Drop the ball, transfer the jackstone to the left hand, pick up another jackstone, and catch the ball after it has bounced once. Proceed as in 1.

6. Sweep the floor: Throw scatters, pick up a jackstone in the fingers, move it back and forth on the floor, as if sweeping, and catch the ball after it bounces once. Proceed as in 1.

7. Dust in the pan: Throw scatters, toss up the ball, move a jackstone a few inches, and catch the ball after it has bounced once. Toss up the ball, pick up the same jackstone, transfer it to the left hand, and catch the ball after it has bounced once. Proceed as in 1.

8. Pump the water: Throw scatters, toss up the ball, pick up a jackstone, and catch the ball. Drop the ball, transfer the jackstone to the left hand, and strike the ball on the same downward stroke after it has bounced once. Catch the ball after it has bounced once. Continue until all the jackstones are picked up in order as in 1.

9. Strike the match: Throw scatters, draw a line on the floor with the jackstone, catch the ball after it has bounced once, and transfer the jackstone to the left hand. Proceed as in 1.

10. Boil the water: Throw scatters, toss up the ball, pick up a jackstone, let the ball bounce twice, catch the ball, and transfer the jackstone to the left hand. Proceed as in 1.

11. Set the table: Throw scatters, toss up the ball, pick up a jackstone, and catch the ball. Toss up the ball, lay down the jackstone a little to the left, and catch the ball. Continue until all have been moved one at a time.

Do not throw scatters as in the other plays, but move the jack-stones to the right a few inches, two at a time. Then move them back to the left, three at a time, and so on. The jackstones are moved back and forth until all are finally moved in one sweep.

12. Eat: Throw scatters, toss up the ball, pick up a jackstone, carry it to the mouth, catch the ball, and transfer the jackstone to the left hand. Proceed as in 1.

13. Clear the table: Throw scatters, toss up the ball, move a jack-stone to the left (do not pick it up), and catch the ball.

Do not throw scatters, but move the jackstones a few inches to the right, two at a time, and proceed as in 11.

14. Knock at the door: Throw the scatters, knock on the floor twice with a jackstone, catch the ball, and transfer the jackstone to the left hand. Proceed as in 1.

15. Ring the bell: This is the same as 14, with the exception that the player touches the floor with the forefinger after picking up the jack-stone, instead of knocking on the floor.

16. Spank the baby: Throw scatters, toss up the ball, pick up a jackstone, and strike it against the left hand. Catch the ball and then transfer the jackstone to the left hand. The jackstones must be held in the left hand throughout the play. Proceed as in 1.

17. Kiss the baby: This is the same as 12. The player must pretend to kiss the jackstone. Proceed the same as in 1.

18. Put the baby in the high chair: Throw scatters, toss up the ball, pick up a jackstone, put it into the left hand, which is held close against the chest like a shelf, and catch the ball after it has bounced once. Proceed as in 1.

19. Put the pigs in the pen: Make a pen by placing the side of the left hand on the floor, leaving an opening between the thumb and the ends of the fingers.

Throw scatters, toss up the ball, push a jackstone into the pen, and catch the ball. Proceed as in 1.

20. Over the fence: Make a fence by holding the side of the hand on the floor.

Throw scatters, toss up the ball, pick up a jackstone, put it over to the left of the fence, and catch the ball.

The left hand must not be moved until the whole play is finished.

Do not throw scatters, but lift the jackstones by twos to the other side of the fence, and so on, transferring the jackstones from one side to the other until all are picked up and moved at one time.

21. Around the world: Throw scatters, toss up the ball, pick up a jackstone, carry it round the ball from left to right (up from the left and down to the right), transfer it to the left hand, and catch the ball after it has bounced once. Proceed as in 1.

22. Back again: Throw scatters, toss up the ball, pick up a jackstone,

carry it around the ball from right to left, transfer it to the left hand and catch the ball after it has bounced once. Proceed as in 1.

23. Snake in the garden: Set the jackstones in a line about four inches apart:

X   X   X   X   X   X

Take the ball in the right hand and with it trace a zigzag path from left to right and back again, in and out between each of the jackstones while saying, "Snake in the garden can't touch me." Do not touch a jackstone with the ball, as this constitutes a miss. Stop on "me," toss up the ball, pick up the nearest jackstone, and catch the ball after it has bounced once. Continue the zigzag path from the point where the jackstone was picked up, and proceed as before until all the jackstones have been picked up. Replace them in a line, equal distance apart, trace a zigzag path between each two jackstones while saying the jingle, and pick up any two that are marked off by the path of the ball at the end of the jingle. For instance, start from the left; go over two jackstones, in between the second and third, under the third and fourth, between the fourth and fifth, and so on. In picking them up either one and two must be taken, three and four, or five and six. They must not be divided unless the tracing of the ball does it. Set the jackstones in a line again and trace a zigzag round three, and so on, until a circle is traced round the whole line and all the jackstones are swept up at once.

Pulling and Pushing Games

War

This is a game suitable only for boys. The four corners of the play space are marked off. The choosers are placed one in each of three corners and choose their players in turn. When the three teams are chosen, all come into the center of the play space; and each tries to put the members of an opposing team into the fourth corner, which is the prison. Any player who has one foot in the prison is in and must remain in thereafter and must not try to pull his opponent in after he has one foot in himself; but if both go in at the same time, both must remain in. The players must not take hold of each other's clothing or strike an opponent. They may pull, push, carry, or drag each other but must not intentionally hurt each other, and only one player may tackle another. They continue the contest until two teams are in prison. The team whose players hold the field the longest wins.

Buck the Indian

This is a boys' game. Two teams face each other and join hands in a line, the stronger players being nearest the head, and the others arranged in order from the head to the foot according to their supposed strength. The head player of one team runs and tries to break through the opponents' line. He must not use his hands but rather throws his weight on the joined hands. If he breaks the line, he takes all the players below the break—the weaker players, and places them as he thinks best in his own line. The head of the opposing team now has his turn, and so on, the players down the line taking turns according to the line-up, and the sides taking turns alternately. The side having the most players at the end wins.

Poison Snake

I.   A chalk circle is drawn on the floor, and the players join hands in a circle about it. Each pulls, endeavoring to make the others step inside the chalk circle. Anyone who steps inside drops out of the game. This continues until only two remain for the final contest. Smaller circles are drawn as the number of players decreases and leaves too few to encircle the larger one. The contest continues until one player wins.

II.   Three or four Indian clubs may be set up in the center of the circle, and the contest proceeds as in I. Any player who knocks a club down is eliminated. The contest continues until one player remains as victor.

58

Catch and Pull Tug of War

This game is suitable only for boys. The players are divided into two groups and stand on either side of a line dividing the field. They try to pull each other over this line. In undertaking this contest the players may catch by the hands or feet, but not by the clothing. While two players may not take hold of an opponent, any number of them may form a chain by taking hold of each other and may pull a similar chain of their opponents into their field. If the line breaks, all the players who are left in the opponents' field belong to them and thereafter work for their side. If a player is pulled across the line by the feet, he is considered the opponents' victim as soon as one foot is over the line.

The team having the largest number of players at the end of the game wins. The time limit is decided by the players.

Red Rover

There are two parallel goals twenty or more feet apart. All the players but one, who is *It*, stand on the starting line. *It* calls "Red Rover, Red Rover, John Smith (naming a player) come over!" The player whose name is called must run to the opposite goal while *It* tries to tag him. If *It* fails, this player is safe at the opposite goal and *It* calls out another player; but if *It* tags him these two join adjacent hands and repeat the call, "Red Rover, etc." The player then called out must break through their joined hands, crawl under, climb over, or push the two players back to the goal that he is trying to reach. These two try to push him back to the starting line. If they succeed or if he has to give up he joins hands with them and *It* calls out another player. If, however, he gets to the goal he is safe.

This continues until all have either joined the taggers or have broken through and are safe at the goal. As the taggers' line grows, a player may break through between any two players.

Kicking Games

Guard the Chair

I. The players stand in a circle with one in the center. A chair or stool is placed also in the center of the circle. Any player may start the game by kicking a basketball with the side of the foot, endeavoring to make it hit the chair, while the center player guards the chair by kicking the ball away from it. He must not take hold of or move the chair. The other players must keep their own places in the circle to avoid confusion and scrambling for the ball; each tries to kick the ball against the chair when it comes his way. When the ball is kicked outside the circle, the players nearest to it may run for it. The one who gets it brings it back to his place and starts it from there. Any player who succeeds in kicking the ball so that it touches the chair becomes guard and exchanges places with the former guard.

II. This is a variant of I, in which the ball is thrown at the chair and the center player tries to prevent it from hitting the chair by striking it with his open palm. The other players try to catch it. A successful catcher or a player who hits the chair with a thrown ball exchanges places with the center player.

Volley Baseball

This game is played according to the rules of *Indoor Baseball,* with the following exceptions: Any number of players under ten or twelve may play on a side. There is no pitcher. The batter places the ball on the home plate, kicks it with the side of the foot, and runs bases as in *Baseball.* Base running is stopped by any player's throwing the ball to the catcher at the home plate. The base runner is put out by the basemen as in *Baseball.* The batter is out when his "batted" ball is caught on the fly.

Stick's Up

This game is often played in the street or on a diamond similar to that used in *Baseball.* The players number off in succession, and kick the stick in turn. One, the goal tender, stands the stick or, better still, a piece of garden hose about eighteen inches long, against the curb.

Number One kicks it as far as he can and runs bases as in *Baseball.* The goal tender runs, gets the stick, sets it up in place as quickly as possible, and calls "Stick's up, John (the name of any runner who is off base)." If caught thus off the base, "John" becomes goal tender, and the goal tender goes last in line.

One runner may force another off base, and the goal tender may call the name of any player who is off the base, always prefacing the name with "Stick's up." Unless he does so, the player is safe. The new goal tender takes his place while the game is in process, and the player whose turn it is may kick the stick any time it is in place. No player may be put out unless the stick is up at the goal when his name is called.

Guard the Gate

The players stand in a circle with hands joined. They kick a basketball *with the side of the foot,* trying to get it outside the circle. Each player guards the space between him and his neighbor on the right, and while trying to protect his own gate, he aims to kick the ball out through that of another player. Any player who lets the ball pass either on his right or between his feet drops out of the game. If the ball strikes him above his knees, the player is not out.

Mother Carey's Chickens Dodge Ball

All but one of the players line up one behind the other, each with both arms about the waist of the one in front of him. The one at the head of the line is Mother Carey, and is the only one in the line who may kick the basketball, which she does to protect the chickens—those forming the line. An odd player runs about and kicks the ball, endeavoring to make it hit the feet of any of the chickens. The line swings about as the players try to avoid being hit. As soon as a player's foot is touched by the ball, he drops out of the line. The game continues until all are out.

Corners Kick

Two teams line up at opposite ends of a gymnasium on goal lines three or four feet from the wall. A basketball is placed midway between the teams. The four end players from both teams run to the center, stand with one foot on the ball, and on a signal try to kick the ball against the wall behind the opponents' line. If they kick it above their opponents' heads, it scores one point; and if between the players, it scores two points. (This scoring is reversed by some players.) The four players continue playing in the center, moving freely about to kick the ball as it is kicked to them by the other players.

The players on the home goal may move anywhere between the goal line and the wall and may join in the play but must not propel the ball in any other way than by kicking it.

Whenever a score is made, the ball is put into play again by the next four players.

Striking Games

Pin Ball

This game is played on a space similar to a baseball diamond. The positions of the batter, pitcher, and catcher are indicated in the accompanying diagram. All the other players are fielders, who take such places as they consider advantageous.

The players are divided into two teams of any number. The object of the batter is to protect the pins, bat the ball, and run between bases and the batter's box. The batter stands with the end of his bat in the box, the pitcher throws the ball aiming at the pins, and the batter bats it as far as possible and, if he thinks he can succeed, runs to first or third base, touches the base with his bat, runs back, and places the end of his bat in the box. Such a run scores one point. He is at liberty to make as many runs as possible, scoring one point for each, but if a pin is knocked down while his bat is out of the box, he is out. The batter is in to bat until he has had three strikes or until one of the pins is knocked down when the end of his bat is out of the box. The pins may be knocked down by a thrown ball or with the ball held in the hand of any player. Should the batter accidentally knock down a pin, he is out. Three out on a side puts the other team in to bat.

The score is kept the same as in *Baseball,* and the number of innings to be played is determined by the players.

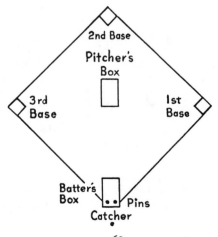

Volley Baseball

This game is played according to the rules of *Indoor Baseball* with the following exceptions: Any number of players under ten or twelve may play on a side. There is no pitcher. The batter tosses the volleyball up, bats it with the fist or open palm, and runs bases as in *Baseball*. The base runner is put out by the basemen as in *Baseball*, and also when his batted ball is caught. Base running is stopped by throwing the ball to the catcher at the home plate.

Piggie in the Hole

All the players are equipped with wand or broomsticks. They form in a circle at least thirty feet in diameter and stand six or more feet apart. All but one dig small holes where they stand, and also a larger one in the center, into which they place a one or two-quart tin can. All then advance to the center, place the end of their sticks under the tin can, and saying, "One, two, three, go!" toss up the can and run for holes, not necessarily their own, into which they put the end of their sticks. The one who is left without a hole tries, by striking the can, to get it into he center hole, which all the others try to prevent by driving the can as far afield as possible; but at any time a player's stick is not in his hole, any player, including the one who is *It*, may take it by getting the end of his stick in it. Without any delay in the process of the game, the player left without a hole becomes *It* and goes into action. When the can lands in the center hole, the game is started again.

Tip Cat

I.   Two or more boys may play, although the number is seldom more than five or six. A five-inch piece of broomstick or a similar stick, sharpened at the ends like a pencil, is called a cat. A hole five or six inches in diameter dug in the ground marks the home plate.

To start the game, a player places the cat so that one end extends over the hole to his left, and with a stick about fifteen inches long, he hits that end of the cat and, as it flies upward, and before it touches the ground, bats it as far as he can. He has three strikes, and every attempt is a strike. If he fails to bat it, he is out, but if he bats it on the first or second strike, he uses his other strikes or strike to bat the cat as far away from the home plate as possible. He may not change the position of the cat before batting it.

When the player has had his three strikes, any player may walk to the cat and throw it at the stick, which the batter holds upright in the hole. If the cat hits the stick or lands within a stick's length of it, the batter is out. If not, he scores as many points as the cat landed stick's length from the hole.

II.   This variant is played by two teams. It is essentially the same as I, with the exception that a team is in to bat until there are three out, whereupon the other team is in to bat.

III.   The game is played by two teams composed of from two to five players. They decide which team is first to bat, draw a circle about two feet in diameter and mark a throwing line about fifteen feet away. Any player from the opponents' team throws the cat from the throwing line, aiming to land it within the circle. The first man to bat, stands beside the circle and may or may not try to bat the cat as it is thrown; but if he tries, it counts as one of his three strikes. However, if he hits it, he may use his other two strikes, batting the cat from where it landed as described in I.

Should the thrower succeed in throwing the cat into the circle, the batter and his team are out. Should the cat land outside the circle, the batter bats as in I. The team is in to bat until there are three out.

Instead of a player from the opponents' team throwing the cat at the stick held upright in the hole, as is described in I, or into the circle, the following alternative is open to any player from the opponents' team who chooses to take the risk: The batter may name the number of leaps he will grant a player to cover the distance from the cat where it last fell and to land within the circle. If a player accepts the challenge and if he succeeds, the batter's team is out. If he fails, the batter's team scores the number of leaps named; the batter bats again and has three strikes.

The players agree upon the score constituting the game.

Shinny

The players are divided into two teams, and each player is equipped with a stick such as a broomstick or a smooth branch of a tree. Each team has a goal at opposite ends of a field three hundred feet long and two hundred feet wide. The goals are six or more feet wide. A knot of wood or a tin can (free from sharp edges) is used as a puck. This is placed midway between the goals, and the teams line up the long way of the field facing each other. Two players, chosen to start the game, stand with their left hands toward their own goals. Simultaneously they touch the ground with the end of the sticks then touch each other's sticks, repeat these movements twice, and each then tries to be first to hit the "puck," driving it toward his own goal. The teams co-operate in getting the puck through the goals. On the final play in making the goal, the puck must be struck, not pushed or kicked.

The sticks must be kept low in hitting, and the players must "shinny on their own sides," that is, they must face the other team unless they are too close to a wall or other barrier, when they may temporarily face the other way to get a fair chance at the puck. After a score is made, they start the game again with two new players in the center. This game may be played on the ice, preferably on a large space.

Swat

The players are seated in a circle. One of them, whom we shall designate as *A*, is given a roll of paper twenty or more inches long firmly tied together. He starts the game by touching one after another of the seated players as he moves around the circle. Eventually, he strikes one of them, whom we shall call *B*, runs and places the roll of paper on a stool that has been placed in the center of the circle, and then runs for his seat. *B* quickly seizes the roll and tries to strike him before he reaches his seat. If *B* succeeds, he replaces the roll on the stool and runs for his own seat while *A* gets the roll and tries to strike him with it. If *A* succeeds, he places the roll on the stool and runs for his seat, pursued by *B*, who picks up the roll and dashes after him. This play goes on until one of the two players gets safely to his seat. The one left in the center starts the game again.

Should the roll fall from the stool at any time, the player who placed it there must replace it before he may take his seat.

Bat Ball

The players are divided into two teams. A chair (or other object) is placed approximately ten feet from the home plate. One team are batters, and the other fielders. The batters number off and bat in turn until there are three out, whereupon the other team come in to bat.

The game starts by Number One batter tossing up a volleyball and batting it up with his hand and then running around the chair and back to the home plate while the fielders try to recover the ball and hit him (with the thrown ball) before he reaches the home plate. The players must not run with the ball.

In case the batter touches the chair as he runs around it, he is out, and the next batter bats, and so on, until there are three out. The two teams then exchange roles. When the teams come in to bat in successive rounds, the players bat in turn as in *Baseball*.

Piggie Move Up

This is a form of baseball in which there is no base running. A pitcher, a catcher, and a batter are selected, and all the other players are fielders. The batter bats the ball, and whoever catches it on the fly is next to bat. In case it is the pitcher, any fielder may come in to pitch, and the former batter becomes a fielder. However, if the batter *hands* the bat to the new batter and he takes it, he loses his turn and the old batter bats again. If a fielder who has caught the ball, and is of course next to bat, throws the ball to the pitcher, he loses his turn to bat. A fielder who has not caught the ball may throw it to the pitcher without penalty.

The players decide whether the batter gets one or two strikes. Everything is a strike. There are no fouls. If the batter fans out, he becomes a fielder; the catcher becomes batter; and the pitcher becomes catcher.

Instead of the fielders volunteering to pitch, they may be numbered and pitch in turn.

Drive the Pig to Market

I. The players are divided into two teams and line up for a relay race. The teams compete in driving a tin can, by striking it with a broomstick or wand, around a goal (any stable object) from thirty to fifty feet from the starting line and back over the starting line. The two head players start on signal and after completing the feat, hand the stick to the next player, who stands ready to receive it. He starts from the place where the can lies and repeats the play, and so on. The team that finishes first wins the game.

II. This is played similarly to I, with the following exceptions: Ten or twelve inch squares of tissue paper or paper bags, blown up and securely tied at the neck, are substituted for the tin can as used in I, and a fan is substituted for the broomstick or wand, and is used to create a breeze as a means of propelling the sheets of paper or bags.

Bat Up Flies

I. The players scatter about. The batter tosses up the ball, bats it toward the group, and the one who catches it on the fly is next to bat. In batting, the batter may use either a bat or his open palm or his fist.

II. This is the same as I with the exception that a bat is used and a pitcher pitches the ball.

Bat Up the Peg

This game is played with a bat approximately three inches wide and twelves inches long and with a square peg four or five inches long and two inches wide, sharpened at the ends like a blunt pencil, and numbered from one to four on the four sides.

The play begins by a player striking the end of the peg from the ground and making it fly upward, then without letting it touch the ground again, batting it up as many times as possible before it falls to the ground. When it falls, the player multiplies the number of times he struck it by the number that is uppermost on the side of the peg, and scores the number of points equivalent to the product.

The players may take turns, or all may be equipped with bats and pegs, and play simultaneously.

Hoop Rolling

A wire hoop approximately three feet in diameter is kept rolling by the player striking it with a stick approximately eighteen inches in length. Players sometimes race with each other.

Hiding Games

Washington Tag

One player, who is *It*, blinds while the others stand close behind him. One of them touches him, whereupon he quickly turns around and says, "Go to the corner and kiss the post"; "Walk chicken steps to the gate"; or anything he chooses. He then guesses who touched him. If his guess is correct, the one who touched him must carry out his order and then become *It*. If he does not guess correctly, he must himself carry out the order and continue to be *It*. While the victim performs the task, the other players run and hide. From this point the game is the same as *Hide and Seek*.

Sardines

While the other players blind and count to the number agreed upon one player hides in a place large enough to hold all the players. The other players separate and hunt for him. Those who find him slip in, unseen by the other players and hide with him. This continues until the last one finds the hiding place.

Mark the Corner

The players are divided into two teams, and a goal is selected. The captain of one team hides all his players in one place while the others blind. He comes back and draws on the ground a plan showing every corner his party turned in going into hiding, even though they may have gone only one foot in a particular direction. The hunters go out together, and all hunt until one of them finds the hiders, whereupon all the players of both teams, with the exception of the captain of the hiders, run for goal. The team that gets one man in first wins and is next to hide.

Baraboo

One player blinds while the other players hide. He then starts out to find the hiders; and since he must not only find but must touch each one, this often means difficult climbing and going through small openings. When a player is touched, he becomes a hunter, but is in honor bound not to find anyone whose hiding place he knew when he was a hider. In each case, however, the original hunter must himself *touch* the players even though they be found by a helper. When the hunters have exhausted their power to find the hiders, the original hunter may call "Baraboo," whereupon all those hiders who hear his voice must answer "Hilow." If they are very near to him, they may answer in subdued tones. The hunting continues until all are found. The last one found is hunter for next time.

Ambassador

The players are divided into two groups, one of which writes a note to a person fairly accessible to both groups but not a member of either. The writers try to deliver the note within a specified time without being discovered by the other group.

The note is written in a safety zone in the presence of both groups and secretly concealed on the person of one of the members of the writers group, to be hidden elsewhere later.

No player may be searched in this zone at any time, and the note may not be hidden there, although it may be carried in on the person of one of the players. The players agree on certain times of the day when the note may not be delivered. The members of the searching group try to find the note or to discover a player in the act of delivering it.

Wolf

One player, the wolf, is given a specified time, such as slow counting from one to fifty, in which to hide. Meanwhile the other players blind at the goal. Following one whom they have chosen as leader, they start out to hunt and continue hunting until they find the wolf; they then come as close as they dare while their leader says, "I spy the woolly, woolly, sheep; I spy the woolly, woolly, dog," and so on, until he chooses to say, "I spy the woolly, woolly, wolf," whereupon all the hunters run for goal chased by the wolf, who tags as many as possible before they reach the goal. Those tagged become wolves and all the wolves hide either separately or together. When the hunters find one of the wolves, the leader repeats the performance as described; and when he says, "I spy the woolly, woolly, wolf," all the hidden wolves jump out of their hiding places and pursue the hunters. The game continues until all are caught.

Blankalilo

This game is similar to *Hare and Hounds.* It is played by two teams. The leading team is given a start in accordance with the possibility of their keeping out of sight of the followers. At intervals the leading team must call "Blankalilo," and the followers must answer similarly. Should the followers lose the "scent," they may call, and the leading team must answer. The aim of the leading team is to make the run and to get back to the home goal without being seen by their followers.

Should the followers catch sight of the leaders, they may run for goal, but must answer the leaders' call and thereby be likely to reveal the fact that they are headed for the home goal. The leaders are then privileged to run for goal also. The team that gets a man to the home goal first wins.

Beckon, or Sheep in My Pen

I.   A goal is selected in relation to the existing boundaries. It may be from thirty to one hundred feet square. One player, the goal tender, blinds while all the other players hide. The final hiding place of every player must be at a point from which, by making slight change of position, he can see some part of the goal. This may be done, for instance, by looking over a wall, around the corner of a house, or even through a knothole.

The hunter gives the hiders the number of counts agreed upon and then starts out to hunt for them. He must call the name of any player whom he sees, and possibly tell where he is, to make sure that he has named the right person. When discovered, the hider must come into goal. This hider then calls "Give me a beckon." One of the other hiders, taking advantage of a moment when the goal tender is not looking his way, may reach out a hand and beckon to him, which gives him the right to slip away and hide again in a new place, if he chooses. The beckon is good until he succeeds in getting away and hiding. This he tries to do when the goal tender is not looking; but should the goal tender actually see him he calls him back, and the hider must come back inside the goal before he tries to escape again. Should several hiders be in at the same time, all who see the beckon may take it for themselves.

The object of the game is for the goal tender to get all the players in to the goal at the same time. To accomplish this he may go outside the goal to hunt but should keep his eye on it meanwhile.

II.   The game is the same as I, with the exception that the goal tender may not go outside the goal to hunt, and that the game ends when all have been called in once, regardless of whether or not they are all in at one time.

Throw the Stick, or Kick the Can

One player is chosen to be *It;* all the others gather at the goal, and one of them throws a stick as far from the goal as possible. While *It* walks, not runs, to get the stick and bring it back and set it up against the goal, the others run and hide. From this point, the game is the same as *Hide and Seek* with the following exceptions: whenever a player is discovered and fails to get in free, he must remain at the goal until another player who succeeds in getting in free throws the stick, whereupon all who are at the goal run and hide while *It* replaces the stick as before. When *It* gets all the players in the goal at the same time, the game ends.

Kick the Can is played the same as *Throw the Stick* except that instead of throwing a stick a tin can is kicked away from the goal.

Run Sheep Run

The players are divided into two groups, one of which blinds at the goal while the other hides in one place. Each side has a captain. The hiders and their captain secretly work out signals by means of which the captain will later try to get his team back to goal in advance of the hunters.

The signals may be somewhat as follows: Red may mean move east; cabbage, move west; sweet potatoes, south; purple, north; beans and corn may mean nothing but may be used to confuse the hunters.

As soon as the hiding group is hidden, its captain returns to the hunters, who all keep together, and goes with them as they hunt, calling out signals to his team, endeavoring to move them as close to the goal as possible while keeping them from being discovered. As soon as one of the hunters sees them, he tells his captain, who then must call "Run sheep run!" Or, if the hiders' captain thinks his team can get to goal first, he may call, whereupon both teams run for goal. The player who gets in first wins for his team.

The winning team is next to hide.

Stillwater

One player blinds at the goal, and the others stand about touching the goal until he begins to count. While he counts to ten, all move as far away from goal as possible, stopping instantly when he calls "Stillwater." He immediately turns around and if he sees any players moving, he sends them back to goal. He blinds and counts to ten again while the others move away. This is repeated until all are out of sight. Once out of sight they run and hide, and he begins hunting immediately. From this point, the game is the same as *Hide and Seek.*

Treasure Hunt

I.   This game requires elaborate preparation by someone who is not sharing in the hunt. First, an object, or possibly something that can be shared by all the players, should be well hidden, and then directions should be written on slips of paper indicating the successive moves each player must make. These are all numbered in succession (1, 2, 3, etc.).

Each hunter's route must be planned separately. At the start of the hunt each is given a slip of paper (marked with a symbol, which has been selected for him). This paper suggests his first move. It might read, "Heat, heat, everywhere, but not a spark to-night," by which is meant the fireplace. Here he finds his next clue, which also bears his symbol, and is numbered "2." It might be some such statement as "Sometimes it's round, sometimes oblong, but it holds eight." This refers to the dining table. Thus he proceeds, and all the other hunters likewise follow their own trail, each hoping to be first to discover the treasure. The number of clues would differ somewhat in relation to the difficulties to be overcome.

Those who plan and referee the hunt, should demand that the hunter who finds the treasure first, present all his papers before permitting him to take the treasure. Because of this requirement, the one who finds the treasure without following his route may be defeated by a player who finds it later and presents all his papers. The number of clues must be the same for every player, and the number be announced at the beginning of the hunt. This game may be played either indoors or out-of-doors.

II. The treasure hunt may also be played by two teams, each following its own route, marked by contrasting colors of paper or by other symbols.

III. The preparation for this game must be made in advance. Articles of various colors and/or forms are placed in such a way as to make them difficult to detect. For example, a silver thimble may be placed on the valve of a radiator; a piece of red yarn may be laid on the petal of a red flower; a postage stamp may be camouflaged by putting it on a piece of tapestry, etc. The players are told what articles are hidden and in what rooms and also that all are in plain sight.

The players start out to hunt at the same time. They avoid giving any help to each other. As soon as the players find all the objects, they announce it and cease hunting.

Instead of giving up, the players should be given every opportunity between other activities to persist in trying to find the hidden objects.

If there are many objects hidden, the players should be given a list, which they may check off as they find them; and a duplicate set of objects may be on display to help the players to distinguish the hidden ones.

Capital Letters

One player is goal tender; the other players stand touching the goal. The goal tender gives the players ten steps or jumps away from the goal, and after these have been taken, calls a letter. Every player then takes as many steps away from the goal as the number of times this letter occurs in his name, while those in whose names the letter does not occur take one step toward the goal.

When the goal tender calls a letter, he immediately counts to ten as rapidly as possible and sends back to the goal all who have not moved one way or the other. These players are not granted the ten steps or jumps allowed the players in beginning the game. The goal tender continues calling letters until he thinks the players can get away and hide. He then calls "Capital letters!" whereupon he blinds at the goal and slowly counts to ten while the other players run and hide. From this point the game is the same as *Hide and Seek*.

Hare and Hounds

This game may be played by two teams or there may be as few as two hares and many more hounds. The game is played in the open country or over another large space.

The hares are given a start in accordance with the difficulties of getting out of sight of the hounds. As a guide to the hounds, the hares scatter bits of paper at intervals of possibly ten steps. In hunting, the hounds are not required to follow this trail although they usually do so.

The hares aim to lead the hounds far from the goal in a cross-country run and to get back to the goal without being seen by the hounds. Should the hounds discover the hares at any time, they try to get back to the goal without being seen by the hares. In case the hares are aware that the hounds have seen them, both run for the goal, and the player who gets there first wins for his team.

Hide and Seek

One player is goal tender, and the others are hiders. The goal tender counts aloud from one to one hundred, or any number agreed upon, and then gives warning by calling "Bushel o' wheat, bushel o' rye, all who aren't ready, holler "I." Any who are not hidden call "I," and after giving them a few moments in which to hide, the goal tender repeats the warning and starts out to hunt the hiders, who watch their chance to run in to goal. A hider must pat the goal and say, "One, two, three for me," before the goal tender can get to goal and do the same, saying, "One, two, three for John" (the hider).

The goal tender may pat the goal for any hider whom he discovers. These hiders must come in to goal and remain inactive to the end of the game, with the exception that they may call out "Lie low," or "Come on in," to the hiders to help them get in free. This continues until all are in. The one first to get in free is goal tender for the repetition of the game after all are in. In case some cannot be found, and the goal tender wishes to give up, he calls "Ally, ally, out are in free!" whereupon the hiders come out of their hiding places.

Hide and Seek in Couples

This game is played the same as *Hide and Seek,* with the exception that all roles are played by couples. In running for goal the couple first reaching goal with hands joined, even though they may have released their hold temporarily, are the victors.

Robbers

The group blind at the goal while two or more players, who are robbers, hide separately. The other players then walk out from the goal, giving a dare to the robbers. When anyone comes near to a robber, he jumps out and tries to tag him. When a player is tagged he is put in the robbers' den where he must stay until all the players have been tagged.

After all the hiding places are known, the robbers find new ones while the players who have not been tagged blind at the goal. The game continues until all are caught.

Racing Games

Apple Eating Race

Any number of apples are placed, each on a sheet of paper, on a goal line. An equal number of players stand on the starting line and on signal run to the goal line, eat an apple, wrap the core in the paper, and run back to the starting line. The player who gets over the starting line first wins.

Automobile Relay Race

The players are divided into two teams and sit tailor-fashion one behind the other, and close together in two lines. On a signal the head player of each line runs around an object (placed approximately twenty-five feet in advance of the head of the line) and back to the second player, takes him by the right hand, and runs with him around the foot of the line, where he himself drops off and sits behind the end player. The second player continues running down the left side of his own line, around the object, and takes the third player by the hand, runs to the foot of the line with him, and drops off at the end. Each player in turn does likewise.

It will be noted that the players sitting in line do not move up as the space in front of them is vacated, which necessitates leaving a space a little longer than the line between the end player and the wall. The race is won when the last player drops into place at the end of the line.

Hand to Hand Race

The players form in two equal lines facing each other about three feet apart. A miscellaneous collection of identical objects are placed on the floor beside the two head players. On a signal the players pass the objects from one to the other down the line to the foot where they are piled on the floor. When the last one has been laid down, the foot players begin passing them back to the head. The line that finishes first wins the race.

Balance Race

The players are divided into two or more equal groups and stand in line, the head players a few feet from an Indian club (anything that stands about fifteen inches high). On a signal, the head players run to the club, stand on the right or left foot, as previously determined and without touching the floor with the hands or the other foot try to touch the top of the club with the end of the nose. These players run back and touch off the second players, and so on until all have had turns. The line that has the fewest failures wins.

74

Rope Relay

Two teams line up facing each other and compete in going through rope rings. Two rings of equal size are made of pieces of express cord barely long enough to go around the hips of the largest player. On a signal the first player in each team goes through the ring, head or feet first, as he chooses, but without help from any other player. The next player picks up the ring and does likewise, and so on. The line that finishes first wins.

Potato Race

I.   When played at picnics and on similar occasions, a dozen or more potatoes are placed several feet apart in two or more parallel rows, and the contestants are lined up, each at the head of his row. On a signal each carries his potatoes, one at a time, to a basket on the starting line. The one who finishes first wins the race.

II.   Players of about equal ability are chosen to race. They are seated on chairs, each facing a row of blocks, bean bags, or any stable objects placed on crosses drawn on the floor three or four feet apart. On a signal each runs and carries the objects one at a time and places them on his chair. When a player gets all his objects on his chair, he immediately puts them back on the crosses again, one at a time. The one who finishes and is seated on his own chair first wins the race.

Dance Relay

An equal number of couples form in two lines and stand behind a starting line. A chair is placed thirty or more feet in front of each line. On a signal, the head couples of each line waltz, or dance any step previously agreed upon, down the hall, around the chair, and back to place. When they have danced back and crossed the starting line, the second couples start, and so on. The line that finishes first wins.

Suitcase Race

Two suitcases are packed with similar articles of clothing, such as, coats, hats, gloves, rubbers, together with an umbrella. Each suitcase contains two outfits, one for a man and one for a woman. Two couples compete in putting on the clothing, closing the suitcase, and carrying it and the open umbrella around the room or over any designated course. They must then take off and repack the clothing. The couple that finishes first wins.

Sense Games

Blindman's Buff

One player volunteers to be the blindman. He is blindfolded, and stands in the midst of the group of players, who move freely about until he signals them to stop. All must stop immediately, and stand still, although they may stoop or move one foot to keep out of reach of the blindman, who is allowed three steps. Should he touch a player, he may have no more than his three steps to take him near enough to the player to enable him to identify him, which he may do by feeling of his clothing and face.

French Blindman's Buff

The players stand in a circle with one player in the center. The circle players join hands and move around until the center player, who has his eyes shut, raps on the floor with a stick which he holds. The circle ceases moving, and the players remain silent. The blindman then points the stick at a player. This player takes the end of the stick in his hand and answers any question the blindman chooses to ask him. Naturally, the blindman tries to ask questions that require a long answer, for he must identify the player by his voice, which may be disguised. The blindman has three guesses, and if he guesses correctly, the other player becomes blindman; if not, the blindman continues until he succeeds.

Still Pond

The players join hands in a circle and move rapidly around one who is blindfolded and stands in the center. When he calls "Still pond, no more moving!" they stand immovable while he tells them the moves they will have to escape him later. He may give them two hops, one leap, and two rolls or any movements and any number he chooses. He then starts out in search of a victim. His steps are not limited; the others use their steps, hops, etc., as they need them to escape him. If he fails to catch anyone or makes a mistake in identifying the one he does catch, he is *It* again; but if he identifies the player correctly, these two exchange places, and the game is begun again.

Beckon, or Silent Circle

The players stand in a circle with one in the center, who shuts his eyes. The leader beckons to a player, who goes in on tiptoe and tries to touch the center player without being heard by him.

The center player listens carefully and points in the direction of any sound he hears. If he points at an approaching player, that player must return to his place, and the leader designates another one to try.

When a player is successful in touching the center player without being heard by him, the two exchange places. The center player continues in the center until someone succeeds in touching him. Naturally, the game must proceed in complete silence.

Dollar, Dollar

The players sit in a circle and pass a silver dollar or half-dollar from one to another while the one in the center, who has as many guesses as he needs, tries to discover who has the coin in his hands. The players sing the following song and keep up a continuous movement of the hands:

1. Dol - lar, dol - lar, how you wan-der, From the one hand to the oth-er;

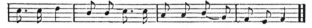

Is it fair, is it fair, To keep { poor Ma - ry / Mrs. Jones } stand-ing there?

The rhythm is as follows: Hands together on the first beat, joining momentarily with the neighbor on either side on the second beat, and so on. If the rhythm is kept, it is more difficult for the one in the center to discover the coin. Whoever is caught with it in his hand or drops it, changes places with the one in the center.

The center player should stand with his eyes closed through ten counts to give the players a chance to start the coin.

Pass the Bean Bag

One player stands in the center, and the others stand close together in a circle with their hands behind them. They pass an object such as a bean bag, from one to the other while the one in the center tries to locate it. He must continue until he succeeds. The one who is caught with it in his hand exchanges places with the one in the center.

Hands Up

The players sit in two equal rows, facing each other. The two players at the head of the lines are captains and are the only ones who may speak without permission. One side has a crumpled bit of paper about the size of a small marble, which the players pass from one to the other behind their backs.

When the opposite captain calls "Hands up!" all close their fists and hold them above their heads. When he calls "Hands down!" all bring their hands to rest on the thighs with the open palms down, and hold the hands in this position.

The captain of the opposite group calls on his players as they raise their hands for permission to guess which hand conceals the paper. One may say, "Mary's right hand." Mary lifts her right hand, and if it is not there, she places her hand behind her and keeps it there until the paper is discovered. Upon its discovery, the captain of the guessing side counts the number of hands that are still down, and his side scores that number of points. If a player speaks without permission, the opposite side scores one point.

The other side now passes the paper. Each group has an equal number of turns, and the one who has the highest score wins.

Up Jenkins

The players are divided into two groups, *A* and *B*, and each chooses a captain. The *A* group passes a coin, usually a twenty-five cent piece, from hand to hand under the table until the *B* captain calls "Up Jenkins," whereupon the *A* group raise their clinched fists above their heads and hold them there until the *B* captain calls "Down Jenkins." All the *A* players immediately bring their hands down with a sharp slap and with their palms flat on the table. The *B* players then guess under which hand the coin is concealed and instruct their captain as to which hand they wish to have removed, endeavoring to leave the one under which the coin is concealed until last. The *B* side scores points equivalent to the number of hands that were removed.

The coin is then given to the *B* side, and the game is repeated.

Jacob and Rachel

I.　　　The players stand with their hands joined in a circle to prevent the two in the center from running outside the circle. Jacob, who is blindfolded, tries to catch Rachel, who has a string of sleigh bells (children's reins) hung around her neck. When Rachel is caught, both choose new players.

II.　　　Instead of wearing the sleigh bells, Rachel may call "Here I am," in response to Jacob's question, "Where art thou?"

III.　　　Both Rachel and Jacob may be blindfolded and omit the sleigh bells and the questions and answers.

Knocking

With the exception of one, all the players shut their eyes while this one knocks distinctly three times on any object and then walks noiselessly away from it. He then tells the others to open their eyes and chooses one, who thinks he knows, to tell what was knocked on. Should he fail, another is chosen. Should the players show confusion, they may shut their eyes again while the knocking is repeated.

Jingle the Keys

The players stand in a circle, with one in the center with his eyes shut. The leader gives keys on a ring to one of the players, who jingles them and then holds them still, whereupon the center player tries to go and get them. If he cannot locate them, he is helped by a slight jingle. When he locates them, the leader nods to another player who says, "Bring them to me." The center player, with his eyes still shut, tries to take them to the one who requested him to do so.

Animal

The players join hands in a circle with one in the center holding a stick. The center player shuts his eyes while the others move rapidly about him until he raps on the floor with the stick, whereupon all stand in place. He points at a player with the stick and asks him to make the sound of an animal, this player takes hold of the end of the stick and imitates any animal he chooses. The center player has three guesses to identify the person who is imitating the animal. If he is successful the two players exchange places; if not, he continues in the center until he succeeds.

A, B, C

I. Two players have a picture between them. The first finds something shown in the picture the name of which begins with the letter "a." It must be a concrete noun and the object must be seen in the picture. For example, he may say, "Arm." The second player now has a turn and may say, "Apron."

The second player now has first turn in finding a "b," and the first player has the second turn. Thus they have first turns alternately. Neither may name anything that has been named by the other even though there be two such objects. The player who completes the alphabet with the fewest omissions wins the game.

The length of time each may have in which to find the object may be determined by the players; but a slow player should not be hurried, as it may so confuse him that he may lose much of the value of the game.

II. Instead of using a picture, the players may name visible objects, or even invisible ones, provided they are in the room. A large group may play, going completely around the group for each letter and giving first turn to each of the players in succession. In this case each keeps his own score.

Colors

I. The players decide on a color and then take turns, each naming an object of that color or a bit of that color found in the room. The same object may not be named twice; and any player who fails to find something within the specified time loses his turn for that round but may join in on the next round. The game continues until no one can find a new bit of the color.

II.   Forms, such as spheres and cylinders, may be substituted for colors.

Travelers

I.   This game is played while traveling. The players make a list of animals usually seen while traveling, and assign points to each. For example: cow, 1 point; horse, 2 points; dog, 3; cat, 5; donkey, 20; and so on. The player who is first to announce that he sees the animal is the only one permitted to score for that particular one. The player who first succeeds in making the prescribed number of points wins the game.

II.   A variant of this game is made by each player trying to complete the alphabet by naming any objects seen. Two players may not use the same object or class of objects seen in the same place. For instance, an apple tree may have a number of apples, but only the player who first claimed it may use it for his letter "a." Apples seen after that particular tree or orchard has been passed may be used. The objects must be claimed in the order of the alphabet.

III.   Instead of traveling, the players may sit by the window and try to complete the alphabet by naming passing objects in alphabetical order seen from the window. Or, they may name stationary objects visible to them from the window.

Peddler

One player is given five or more objects, which he "sells" (distributes) to the others as he walks among them. As soon as a buyer gets an object, he hides it on his person. When all are sold, the seller tries to collect them in the order in which he sold them. If he is unable to collect them, another player who thinks he can do so is chosen.

Stone Teacher

The players sit on the bottom step of a flight of stairs while one, the "teacher" stands facing them. The teacher puts his hands behind him, and shifts a pebble which he holds, from one hand to the other, and then holds his closed fists out in front of the end child, who guesses in which hand the pebble is concealed. If he guesses correctly he moves up a step; if not, he remains where he is. The teacher repeats this for each child. The one who is first to make the trip to the top and back to the bottom step takes the teacher's place, and the teacher sits on the bottom step at the end of the line and joins in the game. The new teacher begins where the former one left off.

Schuster, Schuster

This is played the same as *Stone Teacher* with the following differences: Instead of simply holding out his hands, the child with the pebble places one fist upon the other and, while saying, "Schuster, Schuster; up, down; up, down," alternately changes the position of his fists. The other guesses whether the pebble is up or down.

Button, Button

I.   One player is sent from the room while another gives a button to a third one. All the players clasp their hands together, pretending to conceal the button. The first player is called back, and the others say, "Button, button, who's got the button?" He has three chances to locate the button. If he fails he is *It* again; if he succeeds, he chooses another to take his place.

II.   All are seated in a circle, each player with his hands clasped together. One goes around, pretending to drop the button in each pair of hands as inconspicuously as possible.

When he has gone completely round the circle and dropped the button in one pair of hands, he chooses someone to hunt for it. The hunter may have three guesses. If he is successful, he in turn hides the button. If he fails to find it, the first player chooses another player to try to find it, and so on, until it is found.

Ring on a String

A ring is slipped onto a cord long enough to extend completely around the circle of players, who hold it loosely in both hands and slip the ring from one to another while one in the center tries to locate it. If he succeeds, the one under whose hand it was discovered exchanges places with him.

I Spy

I.   The players choose an object, which they hide after sending one of their number from the room. When this player returns and begins to hunt for the hidden object, the others clap or sing, or both, loudly when he is near the hiding place, and softly when he is far from it, until he finds it. A piano, played loudly or softly, may be substituted for the clapping and singing. Or, the other players may tell the hunter whether he is "hot" or "cold"—near to or far from the object.

II.   The players are divided into two groups by choosing sides. While one group hides an object which the players have agreed upon, the other group blinds, and then hunts for it. A timekeeper notes the exact time it takes the hunters to find it. When it is found, the finders hide it, and the other side hunts.

On the playground or in camp, it may take hours or even days to find a well hidden object.

Huckle Buckle Bean Stalk

The players are divided into two groups by choosing sides. The hiders decide upon a hiding place and hide the object agreed upon, and the hunters begin to hunt. Whenever a player discovers the object, he pretends to continue hunting for a few moments to deceive the other hunters, then takes a seat and says, "Huckle buckle bean stalk."

The game continues until all have found it, whereupon the former hiders become hunters and the former hunters hiders.

Hide the Thimble

One player hides a thimble while all the other players are out of the room. They return and hunt until one finds it, and takes it from its hiding place. This finder becomes hider on the repetition of the game.

Hide the Clock

The players are divided into two equal groups. One group, the hunters, go out of the room while the other group hides a clock in a place where it can be heard but not seen. The hunters may not move anything in hunting for it but must find it by hearing it tick. When a hunter discovers it, he pretends to continue hunting for a few moments to deceive the others and then returns to his place. The others continue to hunt until all have found it. A timekeeper keeps the exact time it takes them to find it. The finders then hide it, and the others hunt.

Hasto Beano

One player hides an object while all the others blind at the goal. When the object is hidden, they begin to hunt for it. The first one to find it calls "Hasto Beano!" and immediately all run for goal while the hider chases and strikes them with his hand. The player who is tagged first is next to hide the object. Should the first hider fail to tag anybody he continues as hider.

Bean Hunt

Beans are hidden about the room. Each player is given a small bag for his beans, and on a signal all begin to hunt. Another signal stops the hunting; and all count the number they have found. The one having the largest number wins.

Changing Places*

I.   Three (or more) players form a circle inside a larger circle of players. The outer circle is given a few seconds to observe the inner circle, and then the players in the outer circle face outward and close their eyes while each of those of the inner circle chooses a substitute

---

*In all observation games such as *Changing* Places, the policy of having all the players, instead of one, observe the situation, and then face outward, increases participation in the effort to remember the matter involved in the game.

from the outer circle with whom he exchanges places, and then himself faces outward. When all are in place, the leader directs the players of the outer circle to face the center and to open their eyes and then chooses one to put the original players back in their places in the inner circle. Should he fail, another tries, and so on, until one succeeds.

II.   The players stand in a circle and, after looking about to see where each is standing, face outward and shut their eyes. As quietly as possible the leader touches two players, who exchange places. When they are in their new places facing outward, the leader directs all the players to face inward and to open their eyes and then chooses one to name and return to their places those who exchanged places.

III.   Within a larger circle of players, two smaller circles of three or more players each are formed. After observing them, the players in the outer circle face outward and shut their eyes, whereupon some of those in the center change into one another's circles. Those forming the outer circle then face the center and open their eyes. One of them is then chosen to put the players back in their respective circles. Should he fail, another player is chosen, and so on, until one succeeds.

IV.   The players stand in a circle, each observing where the others are standing. The leader chooses two players, who shut their eyes while two others leave the room. The two then open their eyes simultaneously, and each tries to be first in naming the players who were sent from the room.

V.   Five players are arranged one on each corner and one in the center of a six or eight foot square. The other players are given a few moments in which to observe where each is standing; then all face outward and shut their eyes while the players in the square change places. All then face the center and open their eyes, and the leader chooses one of them to put those who occupied the square back in their original places. He must not be interrupted while trying to do so; but if he makes a mistake, another player is chosen to correct it.

This game may be made more difficult by having the players stand in a straight line instead of a square.

VI.   Objects with which the leader wishes the children to become familiar, such as flags, objects to be drawn in art classes, etc., may be used as in V instead of children and placed in a smaller space.

Indians Running

Five or more players are sent from the room and are told to run in, one behind the other, and out again, keeping the file intact, while all the other players are watching closely. After they have run out, one of the other players is chosen to tell who was first, second, etc., in the line; or the players may come back not in file formation, and then be arranged in the original file.

Observation

A dozen or more objects are placed on a tray, which is set in the center of the circle of players for ten or fifteen seconds and then covered or removed. The players compete in writing the names of as many of the objects as they can remember. Or a player may be chosen to tell those he remembers.

Who Started the Motion?

The players are seated in a circle. One player is sent from the room while the others select a leader to start the motion. This player is then called back and stands in the center of the circle while he endeavors to discover the leader, whose function it is to make a motion such as tapping his foot, nodding his head, or moving his hand and to change the motion whenever he sees fit. The other players must be on the alert in copying these changes.

When the center player discovers the leader, two other players are chosen to take their roles.

Dog and the Bone

I.   All the players, with the exception of one, the dog, sit on the floor in a circle. The dog sits or lies on the floor in the center of the circle with his eyes shut and with a bone (any object) beside him. One of the players silently signals still another one to steal the bone. If the thief can get the bone and return to his place without being heard by the dog, he becomes the dog; if not, the dog continues until his bone is stolen. Should the dog think he hears the thief, he must point in the direction of the noise; and if the thief has been detected, he returns to his place and another thief is chosen.

II.   This is the same as I, with the exception that when the thief returns to his place with the bone, he hides it behind him and the dog is then told to open his eyes and is given one guess as to who has it. If he succeeds, he continues as the dog; if not, the thief becomes the dog.

Good Morning

The leader blinds the eyes of one player and silently designates another to say, "Good morning" to him. The blindfolded player tries to guess who spoke to him. If he cannot do so, the leader may let him feel the speaker's face and clothing.

When the players are clever enough and know each other well, two may say, "Good morning" at the same time.

Whistle Talk

One player says something by whistling it. For example, he may whistle "It's a nice day," and the others guess what he said. The one who guesses correctly is next to whistle. This may be played by couples, who carry on a conversation.

Interpreting Rhythms

I. Different rhythms are played on the piano while the players clap or beat time with large spikes on horseshoes or with sticks on the floor.

II. Several definite rhythmic beats are played on the piano, and the players try to repeat the rhythm without the piano accompaniment.

III. Different rhythms are played; and the players march, skip, run, or make any bodily movements they choose in rhythm with the music.

IV. Each may interpret the music as in III, and the leader selects one player's movement for all to imitate, and then another's, and so on.

V. The players are given toy percussion instruments, such as, drums, triangles, sticks, bells, and the like, with which to beat time in rhythm with a piano or other musical instrument.

I See Red

I. One player secretly decides upon a color he actually sees and says, "I see red" (or whatever color he has chosen). It is usually agreed that the color must be within the range of vision of all the players or at least be in the room. The other players immediately begin naming red objects which they think may be the one chosen. There is no attempt to have the players take turns, although the guessers should be clearly heard by all the other players. The one who guesses correctly is next to name a color.

II. Materials such as wood, iron, and glass, or the first letter of the name of an object that is within the range of vision of the players may be substituted for colors.

Mystery Man

The players sit or stand in a circle with their hands behind them. One player, the mystery-man, goes around and puts a different object in each pair of hands and then goes around again and asks each in turn what he has in his hand. The player has only one chance to guess, and then shows the object he holds.

Bits of cloth, such as, silk, rayon, wool, and cotton, as well as other articles suited to the ability of the players, and difficult to identify add to the interest in the game.

Magic Music

One player is sent from the room while the other players decide on one or more activities they will require of him. For example, they may ask him to draw down the window shade, and then make a bow. This player is then asked to come back, and as he moves about the room, the group sing a familiar tune and clap continuously—loudly when his movements indicate conformity to their requirements, and softly when contrary to them. When he succeeds in performing the first activity, they applaud loudly, and then tell him there is something else to be done and proceed as before.

Intellectual Games

Who Am I?

Each player represents a person well known to the group. His identity, unknown to himself, is revealed to the other players by the name of the person he represents written on a slip of paper pinned on his back. The players move about and converse with each other as if each were in fact the person he represents, but in such a manner as not to reveal his identity to him. Each player tries to discover his identity.

Culture, or Who Am I?

The group gathers about one player, whom we shall call A, who starts the game by saying, "I am 'F.' " Let us assume that he has chosen to be Benjamin Franklin. Anyone who chooses to do so may begin questioning A. Any player may ask, "Are you a German Emperor?" A may answer, "No, I am not Frederick, one-time Emperor of Germany." Another may ask, "Are you an American inventor?" A may answer, "No, I am not Henry Ford"; and although the questioner had Robert Fulton in mind, this answer is acceptable because A has named an American inventor whose name begins with the letter "F." If the questioner wishes to ask further questions about Fulton, he must re-word his question. The next question may be, "Are you the founder of the English Society of Quakers?" Let us assume that A is unable to name the person referred to and is, therefore, forced to give up. His questioner may now ask a question that will give the questioners needed information but that must be answerable by "Yes" or "No." Therefore, he may ask, "Are you an American Citizen?" A answers, "Yes."

It would seem that the questioners need waste no more questions on persons other than American citizens; but the fact is they do need to do so to force A to give up, thereby enabling them to get more information by asking questions A can answer by "Yes" or "No." For instance, they need to know whether the character is living or dead, whether he is internationally known—a writer, an inventor, a musician, a statesman, etc.—and forcing A to give up enables them to ask such questions. Only when they have sufficient information, such as the character in question is not living, is a writer, a statesman, and is internationally known, is a questioner likely to ask, "Are you Benjamin Franklin?"

If A is Franklin, the game is ended; if not, A continues, and the questioner who asked, "Are you Benjamin Franklin?" may not ask any more questions until *A's* identity is discovered, and the game is begun again. The player who makes the discovery takes *A's* role.

Poets

The players sit in a circle with one in the center who calls a player's name, spins a tin pan, and calls the name of a poet. The player named must name a poem written by this poet before the pan stops spinning. If he fails, he goes to the center and spins the pan; if not, the other player continues.

This may be varied by reversing the order—the center player naming the poem and the other naming the author.

Throwing Light

Two players secretly decide upon a topic of conversation. They then begin conversing on the topic in the presence of the other players. They must not make false statements although they try to mislead the others.

The other players may not ask questions nor do they guess the topic, but rather they join in the conversation, provided they think they know what it is. One player may challenge another at any time; and when this occurs, the person challenged whispers to one of the leaders the topic he thinks is being discussed. If he has guessed correctly, he joins in the conversation; but if not, he is one-third out of the game. The game goes on until all the players are either in the conversing group or out because of having made three unsuccessful attempts to get in.

A player may join in the conversation for some time without arousing suspicion and then be challenged, and rejected if he is mistaken in regard to the topic.

I'm Thinking of Something

The players divide into two or more groups, and each group selects one player to go out of the room. The players who leave the room decide upon a person, an event, or an object and return, each going to another's group. The groups work separately, each trying to be first to discover what was selected, by asking questions in turn. The questions must be answerable by "yes" or "no" only.

Vocabulary, or Guggenheim

Each player is provided with a sheet of paper and a pencil. A word of any length, but preferably of five or six letters, is agreed upon by the players. Each writes this word across the top of the page so that every letter heads a column (see diagram). The players also agree upon the classification of objects which are to be used in the game and they write these in a column on the left-hand side of the page as shown in the following diagram:

Flowers	S Salvia	P Peony	A Aster	C Canna	E Edelweiss
Fruit					
Vegetables					
Birds					
Animals					
Fish					

The players try to fill in as many spaces as possible, one word beginning with each of the letters across the top of the page for each classification given in the left-hand column. When all have filled in as many spaces as possible or have exhausted the alloted time, one person reads his first word, and all who have the same word cross it out. Other players announce their first words, and whenever there are two alike, both are crossed out. This process continues until all duplicated words are eliminated. The player having the largest number of words remaining wins the game.

Anagrams

I. *Dictionary*

Each player draws fifty letters from a pile of anagrams placed face down in the middle of the table. When all are ready, a time limit is set; and all compete in spelling words, leaving them on the table before them, face up. Words once spelled may not be changed. The object is to get the most words.

II. *Stealing Words*

Any number of players sit about a table and draw, in turn, one letter at a time from a pile of anagrams turned face down in the middle of the table. The players keep their letters lying face up before them.

Whenever a player can make a word from the letters he has drawn, he must do so. He may not change his own words; but whenever he can form a different word from the letters of one belonging to another player, he may take it. In changing the word he must use all the letters in the stolen word and he may use any of his own spare letters as well.

It is not considered good form merely to change singular nouns to plural or to change the tense of a verb as a means of changing a stolen word.

III. *Store*

The players gather round a table. They first agree upon the kind of store they will keep (grocery, hardware, drug, etc.). A grocery store is the easiest to begin with.

Fifty or more anagrams are placed face down in the middle of the table. Any player may begin by turning up a letter. He should not turn it in such a way as to permit only himself to see it while it is in his hand; rather, he should turn the face away from himself and quickly withdraw his hand so that all may see it at the same time.

The players try to be first in naming something sold in a grocery store, the name of which begins with the letter turned up, and the letter goes to the person who succeeds. Let us say that the letter "g" is turned up, and one player calls "grapes," another, "ginger," and still another, "garlic." Let us assume that the player who called, "ginger" was first. He takes the letter, and thereafter no player may win a letter on that word; but since no letter was won on the other two words, they may still win letters.

The players take turns in turning up letters until all are won; or in case no one can think of a grocery store commodity for a letter, it is thrown out. The player finishing with the most letters wins the game.

IV. *Tangled Words*

The players agree upon the number of letters to be used in making their words. Each then selects from a pile of anagrams the letters he needs.

When all are ready, each disarranges his letters and passes them on to his neighbor to the left. Each tries to make the word that his neighbor had in mind.

V. *Logomachy*

After four cards are dealt to each of the players and four are turned face up in the center of the board, the players play in turn, each trying to complete words by using one card from his own hand and as many as possible from the center. Whoever completes a word takes the cards used in making it, and the one having the greatest number of cards when all are played wins the game. The cards thus won are not in play again but denote the player's score. The one making the last word takes all the remaining cards. When the four cards are played, four more are dealt to each player, but not to the center.

Hiding Game

Two leaders choose sides. All agree upon a person or an object to be hidden, also upon certain limits for hiding. Let us suppose that they decide to hide one of the players. Those whose turn it is to hide, secretly choose a hiding place but do not actually hide the person. The other players guess where the hiding place is, not in turn, but whenever they like. If they cannot guess correctly, they may ask questions such as "Can he stand erect?" "Is he high or low?" The hiders may give hints such as "He is in 'C' " (the cellar). The place of hiding may or may not be large enough to contain the person hidden.

Alphabet

Two sets of the alphabet are prepared on five-by-seven cards of contrasting colors. The players stand in two lines facing each other on opposite sides of the room. A set of the cards is given each team and distributed among the players. The leader stands at one end of the room and calls a word, for instance, "band." Immediately the players from each team who have the letter required to spell this word run to the end of the room opposite the leader, and stand in line holding the cards up so that they spell out the word. The side first to finish scores one point. The game may consist of a specified number of points or may be concluded at the will of the players.

It is well to prepare in advance a list of words in which the same letter does not occur twice. If there are fewer players than there are letter in the alphabet, the words must be kept within the limitations of the letters in use.

Arithmetic Games

Sets of cards with which the following games may be played are made by printing, one on each card, numbers running from one to one hundred:

I.   The cards are turned face down upon the board. One player turns a card face up; and the next does likewise, whereupon all compete in being first to call the sum of the two numbers. The first to call the correct sum receives the two cards. In case of a tie the cards are turned face down on the board to be used again.

In turning up the cards, the players should turn them quickly, with the face of the card away rather than toward themselves. This gives all a fair chance to see the card at the same time. The game continues until all the cards are used. The player having the most cards wins the game.

II.   The game may also be played by subtracting or multiply the two numbers.

III.   The cards may be sorted so that only those showing multiples of a specific number, three, for example, are used. These are placed face down; and, as each is turned up, as described in I, the players call the number which, multiplied by three (or whatever number was selected as the common multiple), yields the number on the card. Thus if twenty-one is turned up, the player who first calls "Seven" receives the card. The one having the largest number of cards wins the game.

IV.   Two sets of cards may be made by printing large-sized numbers, one on each card, and running from one to any number suitable for the players. The cards are distributed among the players, who are divided into two teams. Each player may have more than one card. All lay their cards before them face up. The leader gives problems in addition, subtraction, or division, and the players holding the cards designating the answer, try to be first to hold up these cards. The one who is first to hold up the correct answer wins a point for his side. For instance, the leader may call "Fifty-six divided by four." The players holding cards number fourteen hold them up. The players may be permitted to hold up two or more cards, the sum of which equals the correct answer to the problem.

Nouns

After supplying the players with paper and pencils, the leader selects a story, poem, or Mother Goose rhyme, which is familiar to the group but he does not disclose the name of his selection. He then reads it silently, and asks the first player to write a concrete noun beginning with the letter with which the first concrete noun in the story begins, the second player the second noun, and so on, until all the nouns in the story have been assigned. A player must not repeat nouns in his own list even though he may be given the same letter more than once. When all are assigned, the leader begins to read aloud, waiting for each one in turn to supply the nouns instead of reading those in the book. Let us suppose "The Three Little Pigs" has been selected and begins, "Once upon a time there were three little pigs who lived with their mother in a pen," etc. The first player has written a noun beginning with "p" (ponies, for example), the next a noun beginning with "m" (master), the next a noun beginning with "p" (piano). The leader reads, "Once upon a time there were three little - - -," whereupon the first player says, "Ponies." The leader continues, "who lived with their 'master' (supplied by the next player) in a 'piano' (supplied by the third player)," etc.

Verbs, descriptive adjectives, or any part of a sentence may be selected instead of nouns.

Spelling Baseball

The class is divided into baseball teams of any number of players. Each team chooses its pitcher and umpire. The pitcher of one team "pitches" the words for the players of the other team. The players stand in line facing the pitcher and spell in turn, beginning at the head of the line. If the first player spells correctly, the pitcher gives a word to the next player. If he fails to spell correctly, it is called an "out" by the umpire. The pitcher gives the same player another word and continues until he spells correctly or until the team has three out, in which case the other team comes in to the "bat."

If the whole team spell correctly once through, they score one run. Let us suppose that there are nine players on the teams and that number seven misspells his word; no run is scored until numbers 8, 9, 1, 2, 3, 4, 5, 6, and 7 have spelled their words correctly.

When the game is played in the schoolroom the umpire holds the spelling-book and decides whether the word is spelled correctly. The pitcher and the umpire should be selected for each period. The words may be taken from any lesson that has been assigned during the term, including the one from the day on which the game is played.

The score may be continued through a month. The teams play in turn; that is, they may stay in until they have three out, even though they continue from day to day. If it is necessary to put difficulties in the way of a clever team, they may be required to pronounce the word, spell it, and pronounce it again.

Blackboard Relay

I.   The players are divided into two or more teams. The leaders in each team start from a starting line, run to the blackboard, write two numbers one under the other, and either add or subtract them, putting down the sum. Each runs back and hands the chalk to the second player, who is on the starting line. He runs to the board and puts a number under this sum and either adds or subtracts the numbers. The game continues until the last player has his turn. He must add or subtract so as to secure a final sum previously determined. For instance, if thirty-five is to be the final number and the figure left by the next to the last player is seventy-seven, the last player must subtract forty-two.

If a player makes a mistake, the next one must correct it before contributing his own number.

II.   This game may be played by having each player contribute one word toward a complete sentence which must be finished by the last player's word, or by the last player regardless of the number of words he uses.

III.   The game may also be played by drawing a picture to which each contributes and which the last player finishes. For instance, the picture may be composed of a house, two trees, a fence, a child, and a dog, which may be as simple or as elaborate as the players care to make them. Each team must fulfil these requirements, the last player adding whatever is needed to complete the picture.

Spell Down

The players are divided into two teams, A and B, and sit facing each other, a few feet apart. The player at the head of line A begins by spelling any word which comes to mind, for example, "boy." The player at the head of line B must spell a word beginning with the last letter of the preceding word, in this case, "y." He might choose to spell "yet." The next player in line A must now spell a word beginning with "t," and the other players continue in the same manner.

Any player who misspells a word, repeats a word that has been used, or hesitates longer than the time agreed upon is out of the game (although he still retains his seat), and the next player in the opposite line has the next turn. He spells a word beginning with the letter the last player failed to use successfully. The team whose players are last to be eliminated wins the game.

As the game proceeds, one player may be pitted against several on the opposing side, but, even so, he may spell them all down.

Passing a stick or any other object from one speller to the next helps to avoid confusion in the order of spelling.

Teakettle

A player leaves the room while the remaining players decide upon two or more words having the same pronunciation but different meanings, for example, steaks, stakes.

The absent player returns, and each of the others in turn makes a statement containing the word but instead of actually using the word subsitutes "teakettle" for it. Thus:

"The teakettles (stakes) were high."

"After the teakettles (stakes) were in his hands, he ordered teakettles (steaks) for his cronies."

"The teakettles (stakes) were driven with terrific blows."

The odd player has as many guesses as there are players. Should he fail to guess correctly, he chooses another to take his place, or he may be required to try again after the group has chosen new words.

Tangled Sentences

Each of the players writes a sentence but instead of putting the words in the proper order disarranges them. For example, the words may read as follows:

"Is propaganda another scandal and one thing still another news?"

The tangled sentences need not necessarily make sense. Untangled, the sentence reads:

"News is one thing, scandal another, and propaganda still another."

The tangled sentences are written out and passed by each player to his neighbor on the right. All compete in being first to make a correct sentence using all the words.

Stock Exchange, or Cross Word Game

Each player draws a large square and divides it into twenty-five small squares as for a crossword puzzle. Each in turn names a letter of the alphabet which all place in their own squares as they choose. In so doing, they try to place the letters so that as many words as possible can be made from them.

In making words, the letters must run consecutively but may be read from left to right, from right to left, upward or downward, or diagonally from the corners. The word may begin and end in any square.

For example, in the following partially filled diagram the word "yearn" on the top tier yields six words: yearn, year, earn, ear, ye, and yea. One diagonal yields four words: night, nigh, gin, and in. The other diagonal yields but one: guy. The players compete in endeavoring to get the most words.

This game may also be played by limiting the words which may be counted to those reading from left to right, top to bottom, and left to the right on all the diagonals. The words may begin in any square.

Y	E	A	R	N
	U		I	
		G		
	H		X	
T				Z

Letter Puzzles

Large letters may be cut from posters. Then after each letter is cut into several pieces and each cut-up letter is enclosed in an envelope, they are distributed among the players, who begin simultaneously and compete in putting the pieces together to make the letter.

Orchestra

The players sit in a circle with one in the center, who plays the fiddle. Each of the other players selects a different instrument and plays it in pantomime continuously whenever the center player plays his fiddle. At any moment the fiddler may begin playing another player's instrument, and that person must immediately begin to fiddle. If the fiddler points to this player before he begins to play the fiddle, he must exchange places with the fiddler. Also, any player whom the fiddler discovers failing to play his instrument when he is playing his fiddle must exchange places with him.

The center player always plays the fiddle but upon exchanging places with another player, takes the instrument that person was playing.

The players may sing a tune, or an accompaniment may be played on a musical instrument.

Rhymes

The players sit in a circle with one in the center. The center player says a word of one syllable and points to someone in the circle, who must give a word that rhymes with it before the one in the center counts ten. Should he fail to give the word within the time allotted, he exchanges places with the center player; but, if he succeeds, the one in the center continues his role. A player who uses a word once used by another player exchanges places with the center player.

Transformation

The players are given pencils and paper and assigned a word to be changed into another word. The process must be that of making a good English word by changing only one letter at a time in each word while keeping them in the proper order. For example, pine changed to pulp might run as follows: pine, pane, pare, pore, pole, poll, pull, pulp.

It is interesting to experiment with words, not knowing whether they can be transformed as undertaken.

Quick Numbers

The players are seated in a semicircle and number off consecutively, Number One being at the head. He starts the game by calling another player's number. The player whose number is called responds immediately with still another number, and so on. The player who fails to call a number before the one who called his number points at him, goes to the foot of the semicircle; and all players below him move up one place, each taking the number of the person whose place he takes. Number One starts the game again by calling a number, and the game proceeds as before. When Number One fails, he goes to the foot of the line, and Number Two takes his place.

The Prince of Paris

The players sit in a semicircle and number off consecutively. The leader is seated at the end to the right and starts the game by saying, "The Prince of Paris has lost his hat. Did you find it, Number Six, sir?" (Naturally, the leader may call on any player.)

Number Six immediately answers, "What sir! I, sir?" The following conversation is continued between the leader and Number Six:

Leader: Yes sir, you sir!

Number Six: No sir, not I sir!

Leader: Who then, sir?

Number Six: Number Ten, sir!

The leader now tries to say, "The Prince of Paris has lost his hat," before Number Ten can say, "What sir! I, sir?" If Number Ten succeeds, he and the leader carry on the identical conversation which took place between Number Six and the leader. Should the leader succeed, he and Number Ten exchange places. Should any player make a mistake in repeating the conversation, he must exchange places with the leader.

Capping Verses

All the players are equipped with pencils and paper. Each player writes one line of an original poem, and passes the paper to his neighbor on his right, who adds another line in meter corresponding to that of the first line. He then folds the paper so that only his line shows, and passes it on to his right-hand neighbor, who adds a line, and so on, until the passing is stopped, and the papers are passed to the next player to be finished, and then passed to the next player to be read by each in turn.

Twenty Questions

While one player is out of the room, the others decide on a person, an event, or an object. The player is called in and allowed to ask twenty questions answerable only by "yes" or "no," which he thinks will enable him to guess what the group has in mind. He has only three guesses to do so. Whether he succeeds or fails, another is chosen to take his place.

Singing Proverbs

The players are divided into any number of small groups. Each group decides upon a proverb, which is broken up so that each member has one or two words. The groups take turns in singing.

One of the players gives the pitch, and at a signal each of the players in that group begins to sing the word or words assigned to him on the same note or to a familiar tune. The others try to guess the proverb. The group that guesses correctly sings its proverb next.

Proverbs

One player leaves the room while the others select a proverb, such as "It is never too late to mend," "Faint heart never won fair lady," "Waste not, want not." The words are then distributed among all the players, who sit in a cricle. Should there be more players than words, the distribution is repeated until all have a word.

The player who left the room returns and, beginning with any player he chooses, asks a question of each in succession. Each must use his word in a sentence, avoiding any emphasis or hesitation that would call attention to it.

The player whose answer discloses the proverb becomes the next questioner.

Geography

The players sit in a circle. One begins by naming a city—Denver, for example. The next player must name a city beginning with "r," the letter with which the first player's word ended. Thus he may say, "Rockford," and so on.

Any player who fails to name a city within a reasonable length of time is permanently out of the game. No name may be used more than once, even though there may be many cities of that name. The game continues until only one remains.

Murderer

I. Any number of persons may play. Slips of paper equal to the number of players, one of which is marked "murderer" and another "detective," are placed in a hat. Each player draws one slip, which he keeps the others from seeing. When all have drawn, the lights are turned out, leaving the room in complete darkness. The players move about, the detective either moving among them or remaining by the light switch.

The murderer takes any player by the throat, whereupon this player stands still, counts to ten silently (to give the murderer time to move from the spot), and then screams. The detective immediately turns on the lights, after which no one is permitted to move, and then proceeds to try to discover the murderer.

He may question any or all of the players in turn and all but the murderer must tell the truth. The only question the detective may not ask is, "Who committed the murder?" Only after he thinks he has sufficient evidence does the detective accuse a person of being the murderer. He may have only three guesses.

II. This version is the same as I, with the exception that a time limit is set for the detective in trying to discover the murderer.

Buzz

The players are seated in a circle. One player starts the game by saying, "One;" the next says, "Two;" the counting proceeding around the circle until the number seven is reached, for which the word "buzz" is substituted.

The players continue counting, always substituting "buzz" for any number in which the digit seven occurs, such as seventeen or twenty-seven. "Buzz" is also substituted for any number which is a multiple of seven, such as fourteen or twenty-one. Upon reaching seventy, the counting proceeds as "buzz-one," "buzz-two," etc. Seventy-seven is "buzz-buzz."

Should a player say "buzz" in the wrong place, give a number when he should have said "buzz," or call a wrong number, he drops out of the game. The counting continues from where the mistake was made. The game proceeds until all are out.

How Is It Like Me?

One player is sent from the room while the group decides upon an object, for example, a chair. He returns and asks each in turn, "How is it like me?" Each answers truthfully. For example the players may say, "It stands straight," "It has a nice back," "It is graceful," etc. He has three guesses to discover the object. If unsuccessful, he goes out again; if he guesses correctly, the person whose answer revealed it becomes *It*.

What Is My Thought Like?

One player thinks of something but does not tell what it is, for instance, his vacation. He asks each of the others in turn what his thought is like, and each answers as he chooses.

After going all around the circle, he tells what his thought was, then goes back and makes each one tell how what he said previously is like the first player's vacation.

Crambo or I'm Thinking of a Word

The players sit in a circle. The first player says, "I'm thinking of a word that rhymes with 'sing' " (any word he chooses that rhymes with the word he has in mind). The player to his left defines a word that rhymes with the word given by the first player, for example, "Is it part of the equipment found in most playgrounds?" The first player answers, "No, it is not 'swing'." The players, in turn, continue defining words that rhyme with "sing," and the first player answers with, "No, it is not 'fling,' 'king,' etc.," until someone defines the word he has in mind. Then he says, "Yes, it is - - - -."

If the player had "ring," as worn on one's finger, in mind, he would say, "No, it is not 'ring'," if he were asked by someone, "Is it the tolling of a bell?" In other words, the definition, not the word, is the determiner. The player who defines the word that the first player has in mind gets the next turn to start the game.

If the player does not guess the word that has been defined, the player who gave the definition begins the game again with another word.

Proper nouns are not permissible, and the word given by the first player must have the same number of syllables as the word of which he is thinking.

Polite Conversation

The players are divided into two groups, each of which chooses a representative and also secretly chooses a word, phrase, or sentence. The two representatives, who do not know each other's word, phrase, or sentence, carry on a polite conversation, each trying to introduce his assignment naturally and simply before the other can introduce his.

Telegrams

The players sit in a circle and each tries to write a clever telegram the words of which begin with the letters of his right-hand neighbor's name. For instance, Smith would require words beginning with the following letters: S——m——i——t——h——. When the telegrams are completed, each passes his on to his right-hand neighbor and each in turn reads the one he received.

My Father Keeps a Grocery Store

The players sit in a circle. One begins by saying, "My father keeps a grocery store and in it he sells - - -." He gives only the initial letter of the commodity he has in mind; i.e., "c" (cinnamon). All call out whatever they think the commodity to be, and the first to guess correctly is the next to lead off.

Name Six

All the players except one, who stands in the center, sit in a circle. The center player closes his eyes while the others pass any small object from one to the other. When the center player claps his hands, the player who is caught with the object in his hands must keep it until the center player points at him and gives him a letter of the alphabet. (No effort is made to hide the object from the center player.)

Then the player who has the object must start it on its way immediately so that it passes through the hands of each of the players in the circle in turn. By the time it returns to him, he must have named six objects, the names of which begin with the letter suggested by the center player.

If the player does not succeed in naming six objects in the time that the object makes the round of the circle, that player must change places with the one in the center.

If the circle is small the object should be passed around two and possibly more times.

Predicament

Each member of the group is given two slips of paper. On one he describes an actual predicament such as: "I had to take a train to meet my 'boy friend,' who was to take me to a formal dance. When I opened my bag, supposed to contain my dress, slippers, etc., I discovered that I had a woman's camping outfit." On the other slip of paper each person tells what he actually did in the predicament. The papers are distributed among the players so that one's predicament and another's solution are together. The players take turns in reading, first the predicament and then the solution.

Singing Syllables

The players sit in a circle. One goes from the room, and the others choose a word, for example, "geographer." The syllables are distributed around the circle; "ge" is assigned to the first player, "og" to the next, and so on, repeating the syllables in order, until all have been assigned a syllable.

Each sings his own syllable over and over to a familiar tune (such as Yankee Doodle or Dixie) that has been agreed upon. The odd player walks about the circle listening to each in turn and trying to piece the word together. He has as many guesses as he wishes.

The game may be made more difficult by having the players change places after the syllables have been given out.

Cross Questions

All but one of the players sit in two rows facing each other. Those directly opposite each other are partners. The odd player asks a question of any player he chooses, but the partner of the player addressed must answer it.

Any player who answers the question addressed to him, or fails to answer the one addressed to his partner, or who answers a factual question incorrectly exchanges places with the questioner.

Finishing Words

The players are divided into two sides and sit in two lines facing each other. The first player holds a stick and, after he spells the first three letters of a word he has in mind, but which he does not disclose, he passes the stick to the player opposite to him. This player must finish a word thus begun, although the word need not be the one the first player had in mind.

Should the second player be unable to finish a word, he passes the stick across to the second player in the opposite side, and he tries to finish the word. Thus the stick is passed from one line to the other and to the players in succession until the word is finished, when the next player begins a new word.

The players who fail push their chairs back and are out of the game although they remain in the group.

How Do You Like It?

The players sit in a circle, and while one player is out of the room, the others choose a word having more than one meaning, for example: "box." The player who was sent from the room returns and asks each of the others in turn, "How do you like it?" If he cannot guess the word after having gone completely round the circle, he may go round again asking, "When do you like it?" and if he is still unable to guess it, he may ask, "Where do you like it?" He has one guess for each question.

Recognition

One player hums or plays a few bars of a number of familiar tunes on a musical instrument, and the other players write the name of the tune, each having been supplied with paper and pencil. They then check to see who has the most correct answers.

Beast, Bird or Fish

I.   The players sit in a circle with one in the center. The center player points at one of the players and says, "Beast, bird or fish?" He then repeats one of these classes, for example, "fish," and counts to ten.

The player at whom he continues to point must name a fish before he finishes counting. Should he fail to do this or should he repeat a name which has already been given, he exchanges places with the one in the center.

II.   The center player says, "Beast, bird or fish?' and adds, "Vulture," for example, whereupon the other player must say, "bird."

The Drawing Game

The players are divided into two or more groups who number off consecutively. Two players act as selectors of an abstract word, such as melancholy, joy, triumphant, generous, kind, energy. The selectors write and secretly show the word they have selected to the Number One player in each group. Each of these players goes into action immediately and with pencil and paper draws a picture, design, or graph for the purpose of revealing the word to his own group, who gather round to watch the result of his efforts. The groups compete in trying to discover the word; and as soon as a group succeeds, the Number Two players are given a new word, and so on until all have had turns.

I Give You a Dog

This game should be played by not more than six or eight players. The players sit in a circle, and the following statement, question, and answer take place among them:

First (to second) : I give you a dog.
Second (to first) : A what?
First (to second) : A dog.
Second (to third) : I give you a dog.
Third (to second) : A what?
Second (to first) : A what?
First (to second) : A dog.
Second (to third) : A dog.
Third (to fourth) : I give you a dog.
Fourth (to third) : A what?
Third (to second) : A what?
Second (to first) : A what?
First (to second) : A dog.

As soon as the first player says, "I give you a dog," to his left-hand neighbor, in starting the game, he immediately turns to his right-hand neighbor and says, "I give you a cat." The cat is relayed simultaneously with the dog, and when they meet, the player involved must send them along in quick succession.

Thus the dog and the cat are relayed from one to another player until both are back where they started.

Stage Coach

One player assigns a name such as, coachman, horses, whip, right front wheel, and other parts of the stage coach to each of the players. He then begins to tell the story of the journey. Every time he mentions a part of the equipage that has been assigned to a player, that player must rise and turn around, and every time he says, "Stage coach" all the players do so. When he says, "The stage coach was upset," all must change places.

Any player who fails to turn around immediately when his name is called or anyone who gets the story-teller's seat when all change places, becomes the story-teller, and must take up the story where the previous story-teller left off.

Clapping Songs

One player claps, or taps with a stick, the rhythm of a familiar song, giving to each syllable the correct time value. The other players try to name the song, and the first one who names it correctly has the next turn.

Guessing Songs

One of the players hums a few notes of a song familiar to the others, who compete in naming the song. The first to succeed has the next turn.

When I Go to California

The players sit in a circle. The first says, "When I go to California, I'm going to take a trunk (or anything he likes)." The second says, "When I go to California, I'm going to take a trunk and a hat box.' The next player takes a trunk, a hat box, and adds something for himself.

The game continues, each player taking in *exact order* all that the others have taken and adding his own object to the list. If a player makes a mistake, he drops out of the game and does not add an object. The game is played until the last one fails.

My Ship Is Coming from London

This game is played the same as in *When I Go to California*, with the exception that the articles are named in alphabetical order. For example, the first player may say, "My ship is coming from London laden with apples." The next player repeats this and may add "beans," and so on until the alphabet is completed. If a player makes a mistake, he drops out of the game and does not add an object. The game continues until the last one fails or until the alphabet is completed.

When My Ship Comes In

This game is similar to *When I Go to California.* The players sit in a circle, and one begins by saying, "When my ship comes in I'll—," but instead of saying, "put on my shoes," for example, he puts on his shoes in pantomime. The next player repeats the words, "When my ship comes in I'll—," repeats the first player's pantomime, and adds his own. Thus he will put on his shoes and perhaps play a flute.

Each player repeats, in order, all that has gone before and adds his own. Any one who makes a mistake is permanently out of the game. The game continues until only one remains.

Concentration

This game is played with a complete deck of cards placed face down in rows upon the table. The aim is to match the cards in pairs —two fives, two aces, etc. The first player turns up a card, lays it face up *in its place,* and then turns up another. If they make a pair, he takes them, turns up two more in the way described, and continues until he fails to make a pair.

When he fails, he turns the cards down *in the order in which he turned them up.* This is done to permit all the players to memorize the cards and their positions. The players continue in turn until all the cards are matched. Quiet and concentration are necessary in playing this game.

The player who has the most cards when all are picked up wins the game.

Ghost

The players sit in a circle, and the first one of them starts off by giving the first letter of a word he has in mind but which he does not disclose. For instance, if his word is "which," he says, "w."

The next player thinks of a word beginning with the letter "w," for instance, "work," and adds the letter "o" to the previous player's "w."

The third player may also have in mind the word "work," in which case he adds to the two letters the letter "r." Should the fourth player add either "d" or "k," thus completing a word—an offense which is to be avoided—he would become a third of a ghost. He may be able to think of another word that his added letter will not finish. For instance, he may think of "worst" and add the letter "s." The fifth player may save himself by thinking of "worship" and adding "h." Had he added "t," he would have completed a word. The game goes on until a player is forced to finish a word, in which case he becomes one-third of a ghost but continues to play.

Had the second player been thinking of the word "well," he

would have added the letter "e" and inadvertently formed the word "we," thus becoming a third of a ghost. In case a player cannot think of a word and has to give up, he is thereby made one-third of a ghost. When a player gives up, the next player continues with the word being spelled. Should anyone think that another is adding a letter without having a word in mind or that he is misspelling a word, he may challenge him. If he is found guilty, he becomes one-third of a ghost; if not, his accuser becomes one-third of a ghost. (The next player then starts a new word.)

This continues until a player has offended three times, and therefore is a complete ghost. He is then out of the spelling but tries to get others to talk to him, and if successful, the victim becomes a whole ghost also. The game continues until all but one are ghosts.

When an offense such as completing a word passes unnoticed until the next player has added a letter, it is too late to penalize the offending player. The articles "a" and "an" are not considered words in this game. Also, some players reject all two-letter words.

Rhythm

The players sit in a circle or around a table. All the players establish 3/4 (1, 2, 3) rhythmic movements as follows: First, pat both hands on table or lap; second, clap hands together; third, snap fingers of right hand or move the hands forward with the palms down and parallel with the table.

The game begins by the first player starting the rhythm, and all the others joining in. Then, on the third beat, the first player says, "Rhythm," and continues without a break. On the following third beat, he gives any letter he chooses to the player on his left. This player gives a word beginning with that letter on the following third beat, and gives a letter to the player on his left on the next third beat. The third player, in turn, gives a word beginning with that letter, and so on.

This continues until a player fails to give a letter or a word on the correct beat, or repeats a word given by another player in the course of the game. When such occurs, he re-establishes the rhythm and begins the game again.

Dramatic Games

Charades

The players divide into two or more groups. Each group selects a word and secretly works out its dramatization, syllable by syllable or in groups of syllables, and then the dramatization of the whole word.

After the acting has been completed, but not before, the other players try to guess the word. Should they be unable to guess it within a reasonable length of time, they may ask to have all or any part of it re-enacted.

The syllables must be dramatized, not merely used on conversation. For example, intermission may be acted as follows: *inter* may be dramatized as an elaborate burial scene; *mission,* as a religious service in a rescue mission; and the whole word as a theatrical performance with much made of the intermission between the acts.

The more elaborate the scenes, conversation, and acting, the more difficult it is for the audience to discover the word.

The Game

The players are divided into two groups, which we shall call *A* and *B*. Each chooses a word that can be acted in pantomime, syllable by syllable or in combinations of syllables, *by one person.*

Let us assume that the *A* group has first turn. The *A's* choose a player from the *B* group and give him the *A* group's word written out, which he is to act in pantomime.

He stands where he can be seen plainly by all the players and holds up his left hand, indicating by the number of fingers the number of syllables in the word. He then holds up one or more fingers of the right hand to indicate which syllable or syllables he is about to act. He must refrain from speaking throughout the whole process. When he finishes each "act" he makes a sweeping gesture with his hands to show that he has finished. He then holds up the fingers of the right hand to indicate the next syllable or syllables he is going to act.

When he has finished all the syllables, the *B* group begins to guess the word, and one of the *A* group keeps time. When the guess of any *B* player indicates that he is "warm," the actor gives him a gesture of encouragement; but when his guess is to the contrary, he gives him a gesture of discouragement.

The actor may be asked to re-enact or to act in another way, any syllable or syllables; and since he is trying to help his own side, he is quite willing to do so. Naturally, he tries to act as accurately as possible. After the *B* group has guessed the word or given up, the time is announced, and the other side has a turn.

Titles of books, songs, plays, slogans, and the like may be substituted for words, but the class from which the selection is made should be announced before the acting begins.

Dumb Crambo

I. The players are divided in two groups, one of which goes out of the room while the other chooses a verb that can be dramatized. The outside group is called back and given a word which rhymes with the verb that has been chosen.

After consulting among themselves, the members of the group that was sent from the room act out the verb they think is the correct one. If it proves to be such, the other group applauds; if not, they shake their heads. The guessing group continues to act out verbs until the correct one is discovered, whereupon this group chooses a verb for the other one to act.

Should a group be forced to give up, that group must continue to act a new word chosen by the other group.

II. This game may be played by sending one player out of the room while the group chooses a verb. He then returns and, after being told a word which rhymes with the verb chosen, acts out verbs of his own choosing until he gets the correct one.

New York

I. The players are divided into two equal groups and stand on parallel goals twenty or more feet apart. The group that has first turn decides on an activity to be acted out, and then advances toward the other side while the following dialogue takes place:

First group: Here we come.
Second group: Where from?
First group: New York.
Second group: What's your trade?
First group: Lemonade.
Second group: Give us some.

The players of the first group come as near to the other group as they dare and, giving the first letters of the words indicating their activity, act it in pantomime. For instance, they may say, "C, T," and individually act out climbing trees, each in his own way. The other players guess what is being acted; and when one of them guesses correctly, the first group run for their goal, and the second group try to tag them. All who are tagged join the taggers' side. Should the second group be unable to guess correctly, the first group choose a new activity and act it out. But should they guess correctly, they choose an activity, and the dialogue is repeated, followed by the acting, as before. Both sides have the same number of turns, and the one having the largest number of players at the end wins.

II.   This is played the same as I, with the exception that there is no dialogue and no pantomime. The first side decides upon the name of a flower, vegetable, city, river, or other class of objects and announces the class to which it belongs, for instance, they may say, "C is a river. The others guess and tag as in I.

Skits and Songs

Titles of dramatizable situations, such as, a millinery shop at Easter time; catching the last bus to get to work in the morning; and meal time in a nursery are written on slips of paper of different color. These slips are then cut into several pieces, shaken up in a hat and distributed among the players, who then seek out their groups by matching the colors of their papers. When all the groups are assembled, one player, acting as master of ceremonies, calls upon the various groups to act their assignments.

Songs may be substituted for dramatizable situations, and may be sung, or sung and dramatized simultaneously. Or, the song may be dramatized by the group, and the other groups try to name it. When they succeed, all the groups join in singing the song together, preferably to piano accompaniment.

Trick Games

A Trip to Europe

The players sit in a circle. One of them, whom we shall call "Smith" starts the game by saying, "I'm going to Europe and I'd like to have all of you go along if you will bring the things I want you to bring. I am going to take a salmon." If the player knows the game, he takes something the name of which begins with the first letter of either his given name or his surname, and is welcomed into the party, but if the player is unacquainted with the game, he may offer to bring something that is not acceptable, and therefore be told regretfully that he cannot go. The game goes on until all discover why they may or may not go on the trip to Europe or until they give up.

Which One?

Two players who know the game co-operate. While one of them is out of the room the other players select five objects and place them in a row, one of which is chosen to be guessed by the player who was sent from the room. This player is called back, and his confederate says, "We have selected one of these objects, and you are to discover which one it is. "As he says this, he casually indicates by a movement of his hand which is number one.

If the group has selected the third object, he may point to any two of the four other objects but the third one to which he points must be the third one in the line. Any of the other players who think they have discovered the trick should be permitted to experiment.

My Grandmother Doesn't Like Tea

One player who knows the game begins by saying, "My grandmother doesn't like tea but she likes coffee." The other players ask if she likes this or that, for example, "Does she like cake?" The first player may answer, "No, but she likes cookies." If there are players in the group who know the game they join with the first player and tell what their grandmothers like or do not like, and as the others discover the reason for these likes and dislikes they also join this group. This continues until all the players have discovered that "grandmother" does not like anything the name of which contains the letter "t," but she does like everything the name of which contains double letters.

This, This One, That, That One

Two players who know the trick co-operate. One of them goes out of the room, and the other lays four objects in a row, one of which is chosen by the group as the one to be guessed.

When the person who is out of the room returns, the questioner points to various objects and asks if it is the one selected, observing the following rules: He points to the objects saying, "We have selected one of these four objects," indicating by pointing which is the first one. This first one he refers to as "this," the second as "this one," and the third as "that," and the fourth as "that one." Let us suppose the one selected is the third one. He may point to any of the others provided he does not attach the right names to them. That is, pointing to the first one, he may say, "Is it that?" But if he points to the third one and says, "Is it that?" his confederate answers, "Yes," knowing that is the correct designation. The others try to discover how the trick is done.

Egyptian Writing

Two players who know the trick co-operate. One goes from the room while the group agrees upon a word, for instance, chair. The player is called in, and his collaborator, who has a stick spells out the word by starting his sentences with the consonants and tapping the vowels with the stick. In spelling "chair" he may start off as follows: "Carefully observe every stroke, now." He writes in the air or on the floor and says, "Have you got that?" He then taps the floor once for the letter "a," writes again, taps the floor three times for "i," writes again and says, "Rather intricate, but he is a clever reader."

(Tapping for the vowels is as follows: one for a, two for e, three for i, four for o, five for u). The reader of Egyptian writing says, "Chair." The other players try to discover the trick.

Wireless

Two people take hold of the ends of a towel or string and swing it round and round between them, ostensibly "to get the air waves going" but in reality to listen for someone to speak. When someone does speak, one of the two asks the other if he got the message. If he is uncertain as to who spoke, he says, "No," and his confederate suggests that they begin again. If he is sure of the identity of the speaker, he says, "Yes," and leaves the room. His confederate gives the "message" to the person who spoke immediately before the other player said he got the message. The "message" may consist of a piece of paper, or anything easily concealed. The player returns and names the person who received the "message." The others try to discover how the trick was done.

Photography

Two players who know the trick co-operate. One goes from the room while the other takes a picture by getting a player's reflection in the bowl of a spoon. The spoon is given to the first player when he returns, and the photographer assumes the pose of the person whose picture was taken, thus enabling the other to identify the person who was photographed. The other players try to discover how the trick was done.

Black Magic

Two players who understand the game work together. One of them is sent from the room while the group decides upon an object, and is then called in. The other player asks whether the object selected is the table, the clock, or any other object; immediately before he names the one selected, he names something that is black in color, thus indicating that the next object he names is the one the group selected. (An object having four legs is sometimes substituted for a black one.) The other players try to discover how the trick is done.

Witch Games

Mother, Mother, the Teakettle is Boiling Over

The mother names the children Monday, Tuesday, etc., using months if there are more than seven children, and stands them in a row. The mother charges Monday or an extra child called the "hired girl" to take good care of the children and goes away. The old witch comes and the following conversation ensues:

Old witch: Let me come in and warm myself.

Monday: No, I won't!

Old witch: Go and get me a light for my pipe.

(Monday goes to get the light, and the witch steals Tuesday.)

All the children: Mother, mother, the teakettle is boiling over!

The mother: Take a spoon and stir it.

Children: We can't find one.

The mother: Look in the pantry.

Children: We can't find it.

The mother: I'll come home then.

(The mother comes home.)

The mother: Where's my Tuesday?

Monday: She went down the crooked lane.

(Mother walks zigzag.)

Mother: She isn't there.

(This continues as long as the resourcefulness and enthusiasm hold out, the children suggesting bow-legged street, the singing street, canary-bird street, hands-and-knees street, etc., each of which the mother tries.)

Then Monday tells the mother that Tuesday is in the pantry, down cellar, etc., and at last says, "The old witch took her." The mother beats Monday, tells her to take care of the other children, and goes away. The children repeat the whole performance until all are stolen. The old witch makes the children into pies and places them in order of the days of the week. The mother knocks at the door of the witch's house.

Mother: Let me come in.

Old witch: Your shoes are too dirty.

Mother: I'll take them off.

Old witch: Your stockings are too dirty.

Mother: I'll take them off.

Old witch: Your feet are too dirty.

111

Mother: I'll cut them off.

Old witch: You'll get blood on my floor.

Mother: I'll wrap them up in gold paper and sit in a gold chair.

Old witch: Come in.

Mother: Have you an apple pie?

(Old witch answers truthfully, yes or no. In case she has one she points to it; otherwise, the mother asks for another pie and continues until she finds one.)

Mother: This is too sour (tasting it).

Old witch: I'll put some sugar in it (pretends to do so).

Mother: It's too sweet.

Old witch: I'll take some sugar out (pretends to do so).

(The mother may find other imperfections in the pie, which the witch remedies.)

Mother: This tastes like my———(counts down the line to find what day it is) Thursday!

The mother takes Thursday by the hand and runs home with her. The witch chases them but never catches them. This is repeated until all the children are home again.

Chickie, My Chickie, My Craney Crow

The children mark off a space for their home; the old witch comes along, and they follow her chanting, "Chickie, my chickie, my craney crow went to the well to wash her toe. What time is it old witch?" The witch answers, "Six o'clock" (any time she chooses). They repeat the whole until she says, "Twelve o'clock," whereupon all run for home while she tags as many as possible and puts them in her house. The whole is repeated until all are tagged. The last one caught is witch for the next time.

Grand Mammy Tipsy Toe

The mother gives each of the children a blade of grass and says, "Now you sew your clothes and don't go out after the old witch." They sew; the mother goes away and is transformed into a witch. She hobbles back in front of the house. "Oh, there's the old witch!" the children cry and go out tagging after her as she hobbles along. They chant, "Grand mammy tipsy toe, lost my needle and cannot sew." They repeat this until she turns and tags as many of them as possible as they run for home. All she catches, she put in her den. The whole performance is repeated until all are caught.

Midnight

The children follow the old witch and at intervals say, "What time is it, old witch?" She replies, giving them various times, and eventually says, "Midnight!" whereupon the children run for home and the old witch tags as many as possible and puts those she catches in her den. This continues until all are tagged.

Old Mother Witch

I.   The children mark off a space for their home. The old witch comes by, and they follow her, chanting, "Old Mother Witch fell in the ditch, picked up a penny and thought she was rich." They repeat this as they tag along after the witch until she turns and faces them saying, "Whose children are you?" They answer any name, such as "Mrs. Jones's" or any name that nonsense suggests. They proceed as before until she again turns and asks the same question, to which the children reply with new names. This goes on until they answer, "Yours." They run for home while the old witch tags as many as possible and puts those caught in her den. They repeat the game, and when all are caught the old witch cuts them up and makes soup or grinds them up into sausage.

II.   This is the same as I with the exception that after all are tagged the old witch then goes around taking one's arm, another's leg, etc., to make soup. After she has cut a piece from each child, the old witch runs and the children all try to tag her. The one who succeeds becomes the witch.

Games Requiring Voluntary Control
of Impulses

Fool Teacher

All the players but one, the teacher, stand in a semicircle with arms folded. The teacher stands facing them, about fifteen feet away, and throws the ball to one of them or makes a feint of doing so. The point of the game is for the teacher to make a feint at throwing the ball to a player and make him unfold his arms. If he offends in even a slight degree he must go last, that is, he must go to the end of the line designated as the foot. On the other hand, if he catches a ball that is actually thrown, he throws it back to the teacher or makes a feint at doing so. The teacher must stand with arms folded and should he unfold them on a feint or fail to catch a thrown ball, he goes last, and the player at the head of the line becomes teacher.

Birds Fly

All the players stand in a circle with one in the center, and imitate the center player, who says, "Birds fly" (all move arms up and down in imitation of flying), "Geese fly," etc. When the center player names something that does not fly, such as horses, he continues to make flying movements, but anyone whom he sees "flying" must change places with him. Also, any player who fails to "fly" when something that does fly, such as a bird or an insect, is named, must exchange places with the center player, provided the center player discovers that he is not "flying."

Jerusalem, Jericho

The players stand in a circle with one in the center, who bows every time he says, "Jerusalem" or "Jericho." The others must bow on "Jerusalem," but any one the center player catches bowing on "Jericho" or failing to bow on "Jerusalem" changes places with him. The center player draws out the first syllable of "Jerusalem" and "Jericho" to catch the other players.

Fishing, Fishing

The players sit about informally in a semicircle, each with a forfeit (any small object) in his hand. One player is the fisherman; the following conversation takes place:

Fisherman: Fishing fishing all the day.
Players: What did you catch?
Fisherman: Fly, spy.

114

Players: What did it say?

Fisherman: This and that and all let go (or hold fast).

The fisherman lets go of his forfeit when he says, "Let go," but the other players must hold fast to theirs. Those who fail to do so, give their forfeits to the fisherman and drop out of the game. This continues until only one remains. The fisherman then stands behind this last player and holds up the forfeits one by one saying, "Heavy, heavy hangs over thy head." The other player asks, "Fine (a boy's forfeit) or superfine (a girl's forfeit)?" The fisherman answers correctly. The other player then names the feat which the owner of the forfeit must perform to get back his forfeit. This is repeated for each player.

Red Light, or Cheese It

I.   All the players line up on the starting line, with one who is *"It,"* fifteen or more feet ahead. All face in the same direction and move forward while *It* counts any number up to ten and adds, "cheese it," i.e., "One, two, three, four, five, cheese it!" Immediately after saying, "cheese it," *It* turns about and sends back to the starting line any players whom he sees moving even slightly. He does not begin again until all the offenders are on the starting line ready to begin. This continues until the last one is over the goal.

II.   The game is the same as I, with the exception that when the first player gets over the goal line he becames *It,* and the game starts again.

Contest for Places and Similar Games

Numbers Change

I.   The players sit in chairs in a circle with one player in the center. They number off consecutively, including the one in the center. The center player calls any two numbers, and the players having these numbers immediately change places, while the center player tries to get one of the chairs. If he succeeds, the one left without a chair takes the center player's place; if not, he continues in the center until he does succeed.

II.   This is played the same as I, with the exception that the center player is blindfolded and may either tag one of the players as they change places or may get one of their chairs.

Parcel Post

The players sit in a circle, with one in the center. One player goes around the circle and assigns to each player a different name of a city. The one in the center may say, "I am sending a package from New York to Toronto," whereupon the two "cities" exchange places, during which he tries to get one of their places. If he succeeds, the one left without a seat takes the center player's place; if not, he continues as the center player. Should these cities not have been assigned, he calls others until he succeeds in naming two that have been assigned.

Wink

Half the players sit in chairs in a circle with one extra chair vacant, and a player stands behind every chair. The one with the empty chair winks or nods his head at any seated player, who immediately tries to escape before the person behind his chair tags him. If he gets away, he occupies the vacant chair but, if tagged, he must remain in his own chair. The object is to keep one's chair occupied.

Fruit Basket

I.   The players are seated in a circle. There is one less chair than there are players. One player goes around the circle and whispers the name of a different fruit to each of them, and takes one for himself. One of the players is chosen to stand in the center, and call the names of two fruits, and provided these fruits have been assigned, the two players immediately change places. The center player tries to get one of their places for himself. The one left without a chair becomes the center player.

At any time the center player may say, "The fruit basket is upset," whereupon all must change places. This gives the center player a better chance to obtain one of the places.

II.   The players are named as in I, and the one in the center calls the name of a fruit three times, as rapidly as possible. The player who has been assigned that fruit must respond by calling the name himself before the first player finishes, otherwise these two players exchange places. For example, if the center player calls "apples, apples, apples," the player who has been assigned apples must say, "apples" before the center player has said it three times. The center player must stay in the center until he catches someone.

How Do You Like Your Neighbor?

The players sit in a circle, with one in the center. They number consecutively, including the center player. The center player goes up to any one of the other players and asks, "How do you like your neighbor?" He may answer, "Very well," in which case all the players must change seats, or he may say, "Not at all," whereupon the questioner asks, "Whom would you rather have?" He may say, "Numbers Six and Thirteen" (any numbers). These two numbers must then exchange seats with the two who sit on either side of the person who named them. During the exchange, the questioner tries to get a seat. The one left without a seat is the next questioner.

Going to Jerusalem, or Musical Chairs

I.   A row of chairs is placed down the center of the room so that they face alternately in opposite directions. There should be one chair less than the number of players. At the beginning of the game the players are all seated except one. A march is played, and when the music begins, all the players rise and march around the chairs. At any moment the music may be stopped abruptly, whereupon all players scramble for seats, but in doing so, they must not pull the chairs out of place.

The one who is left without a seat takes a chair away from the end of the line and is thenceforth out of the game. This procedure continues until only two players are competing for one chair, and the one who secures it is the winner.

Instead of removing chairs, the player who is left without a chair may sit on any chair he chooses and remains seated while the others march around. In this way the chairs are filled one by one until the game ends.

II.   Any objects may be substituted for chairs and placed in a line on the floor about a foot and a half apart. There should be one more player than there are objects. The players march around the line the same as when chairs are used, and each tries to snatch an object when the music stops. The one who fails, takes the object from one end and drops out of the game. This continues until the last two players compete for the last object.

Ocean Wave

The players arrange their chairs close together in a circle. One player then goes into the center, which leaves one vacant chair. The center player calls "Shift right (or left)" and changes the call whenever he wishes. The players endeavor to keep the chair on the right or left occupied while shifting as directed. In the meantime the center player tries to get a seat. Whoever is at fault in case he succeeds exchanges places with him.

Newspaper March

Newspapers are laid about three feet apart in a large circle about a large room, or in a path through several rooms. The players march in single file over this path and in rhythm with the music. The pianist stops suddenly as in the game of *Going to Jerusalem,* and all, any part of whose feet are touching paper, are out of the game and must go into the center, where they watch for offenders. Each marcher watches the one in front of him also. The game continues until only one remains.

Poison

The players stand in a circle and pass an object from one to another while the piano is being played. Whoever has it when the music stops is "poisoned" and drops out of the game. However, he may try to save himself by passing the object to the next player even after the music stops and if the latter takes it, *he* is out.

If the group is large, four or five objects may be started at different places in the circle to make the game move more quickly, and when the circle is reduced to ten or fifteen players, all but one of the objects may be taken out.

Squirrels in Trees

The players are scattered about in couples, who join both hands making a hollow tree in which a third player, the squirrel, stands. One odd player is without a tree. The leader gives a signal, whereupon all the squirrels must leave their trees and find new ones. The odd player tries to get a tree, and if he succeeds, one of the others will be left homeless. After a few repetitions of the game, the squirrels become part of the tree and one of those forming the tree becomes a squirrel.

Moving Day

By joining both hands the players make houses, which are scattered about the room. A third player occupies each of the houses and one player is homeless. The leader claps his hands or uses any signal as agreed, whereupon all the occupants of the houses must move into another house. The homeless player tries to get a house. After a few repetitions of the game one of the occupants exchanges places with one of the players making the house. This is repeated until all have been occupants of a house.

The Fish Game

Couples sit side by side in chairs set here and there about the room. Each couple secretly selects the name of a fish. Two players who are without chairs, are whales, and walk in and out among the seated players calling the names of fish. (If the group is large it is advisable to have each repeat the other's call immediately, to make sure that all the players hear it.) Whenever a name that has been selected by any of the couples is called, those couples fall in line behind the whales. Thereafter they may suggest names to the whales, although they may not themselves call them.

This continues until the whales can guess no more, whereupon they call "The ocean is calm," and all the seated couples fall in line. The whales lead them about at will and finally call "The ocean is stormy," and all run for seats, the couples keeping together.

Should one person reach two chairs without his partner and should a couple then claim them, he must give up to the couple. The couple left without chairs are whales the next time. If the group is large, it is advisable to have the piano played while they all march about in line. When the music stops, all run for seats.

Come Along

The players stand in a circle with the left hand extended, and the pianist plays music suitable for running. One player runs around outside the circle and takes anyone he chooses by the hand; they continue running, and the second player picks up another, and so on, until there is a line as long as the leader chooses to make it. He then leads the line outside of and away from the circle, continues running until music stops, when all release hands and run for their own places. The first one in place is the leader for the repetition of the game.

Crosses

The players form a circle. A number of crosses, possibly eight or ten are marked on the floor, inside the circle. Players, numbering one more than the crosses, are chosen to skip about in the center. They continue until the music stops, then run and stand on the crosses. The player who is left without a cross chooses another from the circle to take his place while he joins the circle, and the game continues. To finish the game, the player who fails to get a cross erases one from the floor and joins the circle. This continues until only two players and one cross remain. The one who first gets a foot on the cross when the music stops wins.

Numbers Change in Line

The players stand in line in flank formation and number off consecutively. They then change places to mix up the numbers. One player who is *It,* stands about fifteen feet from and facing the line. He calls two numbers, and the two players whose numbers were called must immediately exchange places. In the meantime he tries to get one of their places. If he succeeds, the person who is left without a place is *It;* if he fails, he continues to be *It.*

Spin the Platter

The players sit in a circle and number off consecutively. One goes into the center and spins the tin pan, calling a number as it starts spinning. The player whose number was called runs and catches the pan before it falls to the floor. If he fails, he pays a forfeit (gives up a piece of jewelry or anything he has at hand) and is next to spin the pan. When a sufficient number of forfeits are collected, they are redeemed as follows:

Two players volunteer, one to select the forfeits and the other to determine how they shall be redeemed. The former stands behind the latter and holding one of the forfeits behind him and above his head so that he cannot see it, the following conversation takes place:

First player: Heavy, heavy, hangs over thy head.

Second player: Fine or superfine?

First player: Fine (if the forfeit belongs to a boy) ; superfine (if to a girl). What shall the owner do to redeem it?

Second player: He (or she) shall (names some fun-provoking performance which the owner straightway executes), and subsequently is given his forfeit.

This is repeated for every player who contributed a forfeit.

Pussy Wants a Corner

All the players, with the exception of one, the pussy, stand on crosses marked on the floor, or corners agreed upon before the game begins. The pussy goes round saying to anyone he chooses, "Pussy wants a corner." This player answers, "Next door neighbor." In the meantime the players give the pussy a dare by changing places, during which he tries to get a corner. Should he succeed, the one who is left without a corner becomes pussy.

Miscellaneous Games

Rattlesnake

The players join hands in a line. The one at the head stands with the right hand on a wall or other object, while the last player at the opposite end leads the line of players between the head player and the one on this player's left. As the line passes under his arm, the second player turns about, bringing his right arm over his own left shoulder, and stands on place.

The end player continues to draw line between each two players until all are wound up in a chain. The head player and the one at the opposite end then join hands in the same way, and the circle runs or skips about until it breaks up.

While playing, the children chant the spelled-out word, "R-a-t-t-l-e-s-n-a-k-e" and then pronounce it, and continue this throughout the game.

Hul-Gul

The players sit or walk about, each with small objects such as seeds or marbles concealed in one cupped palm covered with the other hand. Selecting as many as he wishes to risk, a player approaches another, rattles the contents of his hands and says, "Hul-gul." The second player takes in his hand the number he thinks will equal those of the first player and then guesses the number he thinks the first player holds. Both then show their hands, and if the second player has guessed correctly, he gets the whole content of the first player's hand; but if not, the first player finds the difference between the number they each hold, and then the second player pays the other one the difference between that sum and the number he guessed. For example, if the first player had held eight objects and the second had held four and had guessed five, he would subtract four from eight and pay the first player the difference between that sum, in this case four, and the number he guessed (five).

This rule is followed regardless of which player holds the larger number.

Queen Dido Is Dead

The players sit in a circle, and one of them says to his neighbor, "Queen Dido is dead." His neighbor asks, "How did she die?" The first player answers, "She died doing this," making a movement such as tapping his foot, which all the other players copy and repeat continuously.

121

This conversation is repeated by the second and third players, the second one adding another movement, and so on, until no more movements can be made simultaneously.

Matching Cards for Partners

Playing cards, cut into four pieces, along not too obvious lines, may be distributed among the players. Piecing together the card may be an effective way of getting strangers acquainted or of getting them into groups for games. Cutting the cards into two pieces facilitates the getting of partners.

"White Elephant" Christmas Party

While this is not strictly a game, it may well be included with games. Each guest selects from his possessions something he considers a "white elephant," and wraps it up to look like a Christmas present. When all are assembled in one heap, each guest selects one package, and unwraps it secretly

If it suits him, he keeps it; if not, he rewraps it, returns it, and selects another from those rejected by the others. This continues until each either gets something he wants or is compelled to take what is left.

Jackknife Baseball

The equipment needed for this game is a jackknife with two sharp blades, and a board (or turf). The larger blade should be half open and the smaller one completely open.

The play begins by setting the point of the larger blade in the board, and flipping the knife upward endeavoring to make one of the blades stick in the board. If either blade sticks so that the player can get four fingers between the blade or the handle and the board, he scores a home-run; if three fingers, a third base; two fingers, second base, and one finger, first base. If the knife falls on its back, he scores a home-run, and if on its side he is out.

For two players the game is as follows: The players are A and B. A throws first, continuing until he throws an out. For instance, let us suppose that he throws a two-base throw followed by a home run, he scores two runs. He then throws a three-base throw followed by an out. His man on third base does not score. B now throws. Let us suppose that he throws a home-run; next he throws a three-base throw followed by a first-base throw; and he follows this with a three-base throw. This forces the man on first and the one on third home and leaves a man on third, which scores two runs. He next throws a home-run, raising his score to five. He then throws an out. A now throws, and the game proceeds through nine innings.

For eight players the game is as follows: Let us suppose A, B, C, and D to be the first team and E, F, G, and H to be the second team. The players throw in turn as they bat in *Baseball*. Thus, A throws until he is out. Let us suppose that he throws a three-base throw followed by an out. There is a man on third base, and it is B's turn to throw. B throws a second base throw and does not score. C throws a home-run, which forces the man on second and the one on third base home. Thus C scores three runs. The first team continues until it has three out. Let us assume that D has not thrown and therefore will have first turn in the next inning. The second team now throws and continues until it has three out. The teams play nine innings and the one having the most runs wins the game.

Mumblety-peg

This game is played on the ground (or on a board) with a pocketknife, one blade of which is open. The players take turns throwing the knife from various positions endeavoring to make the point of the blade stick in the ground (or board). The one who finishes all the plays first drives a peg into the ground with the handle of the knife, and to do so has three strokes with his eyes open and three with them shut. His opponent must draw it out with his teeth.

The following are the plays:

1. Lay the knife on the right palm with the blade parallel with the fingers and the point extending an inch or more beyond the ends of the fingers. From this position throw it upward so that it turns over and sticks into the ground.

Repeat the same play with the left hand.

2. Repeat 1 with the knife laid on the back of the hand.

3. Double up the right fist and lay the knife across the fingers with the handle toward the little finger, turn the hand over, and throw the knife to the left.

Repeat the same play with the left hand, throwing the knife to the right.

4. Rest the point of the knife on the left knee and, with the right forefinger on the end of the handle, flip the knife over so that it sticks in the ground.

Repeat the same play from the right knee with the left hand.

5. Take the tip of the blade between the thumb and each of the fingers of the right hand in turn and throw it away from the body.

6. Rest the point of the blade on the left elbow and with the right forefinger on the end of the handle throw the knife as in 4.

Repeat the same play with the right elbow and the left hand.

7. Hold the tip of the blade between the right thumb and forefinger with the end of the handle against the chin and throw the knife forward.

Repeat from the mouth, nose, cheeks, eyes, forehead, and ears. In throwing from the ears, the lobe of the right ear is held in the fingers of the left hand, and the knife is thrown by the right hand from the left ear. In crossing the arms, the right arm must be underneath the left.

Repeat the same play with the left hand.

8. Rest the point of the blade on a folded handkerchief on the top of the head, and with the right forefinger on the tip of the handle throw the knife forward.

Repeat the same play with the left hand.

9. Hold the tip of the blade between the thumb and first finger and throw it backward over the head with the right hand.

Repeat the same play with the left hand.

10. Spin the platter: Catch the tip of the blade under the thumbnail of the right hand and rest the blade on the right forefinger. Throw the knife toward the body; and, as it starts to turn, hit it with the right hand and turn it away from the body.

11. Break the devil's neck: Hold the knife with the blade interlaced between the first three fingers of the left hand with the middle finger on top and the handle toward the right, then hit the handle, making the knife turn over to the right.

Index

	PAGE
A, B, C, I, II.	79
Alphabet	90
Ambassador	68
Anagrams:	
Dictionary	88
Logomachy	89
Stealing Words	88
Store	88
Tangled Words	89
Animal	79
Ante-Ante-I-Over	35
Apple Eating Race.	74
Arithmetic Games, I, II, III, IV	90
Arrow Chase	7
Automobile Relay Race.	74
Balance Race	74
Ball Drill	54
Baraboo	67
Bat Ball	65
Battle Ball	40
Bat Up Flies, I, II.	66
Bat Up the Peg.	66
Bean Bag Board.	46
Bean Hunt	82
Beast Bird or Fish, I, II.	101
Beckon, or Sheep in My Pen, I, II.	69
Beckon, or Silent Circle.	76
Bird Hunter	45
Birds Fly	114
Black and White, or Day and Night	11
Black and White Stoop Tag, or Stoop Tag, I, II.	20
Blackboard Baseball	39
Blackboard Relay, I, II, III.	92
Black Magic	110
Black Tom	12
Blankalilo	68
Blindman's Buff	76
Bounce into a Box.	54
Bounce over and Back.	50
Bounce Up Flies.	54
Bowling	42
Bowl into a Circle.	46
Bowl out of a Circle.	46
Buck the Indian.	58
Bull in the Ring.	16
Bunny in the Hole, I, II.	45
Button, Button, I, II.	81
Buzz	97
Call Ball	37, 51
Capital Letters	71
Capping Verses	96
Captain Ball	34

	PAGE
Cat and Rat.	20
Catch and Pull Tug of War.	59
Cats and Rats.	20
Center Base	17
Center Catch	34
Center Club Bowl.	45
Center Dodge	45
Changing Places, I, II, III, IV, V, VI	82
Charades,	105
Cheese It, or Red Light, I, II.	115
Chickie, My Chickie, My Craney Crow	112
Circle Ball	38
Circle Stride, I, II.	41
Clapping Songs	102
Colors, I, II.	79
Come Along	119
Concentration	103
Concentric Circles Target.	47
Corners Kick	61
Couple Tag, I, II.	12
Crambo, or I'm Thinking of a Word	98
Crooks and Cranes.	12
Crosses	119
Cross Questions	100
Cross Tag	20
Cross Word Game, or Stock Exchange	93
Culture, or Who Am I?	86
Cut the Pie, or Fox and Geese.	15
Dance Relay	75
Day and Night, or Black and White	11
Dodge Ball, I, II.	40
Dog and the Bone, I, II.	84
Dollar, Dollar	77
Don't Hit	47
Drawing Game, The.	101
Drive the Pig to Market, I, II.	66
Drop the Handkerchief.	9
Drop the Handkerchief in Couples	10
Duck on a Rock.	43
Dumb Crambo, I, II.	106
Eagle and Birds.	13
Egyptian Writing	109
Finishing Words	100
Fishing, Fishing	114
Fish Game, The.	119
Fish Net	16
Five Back	43
Fool Teacher	114
Fox and Chickens.	17
Fox and Geese, or Cut the Pie.	15

125

PAGE

Fox, Fox, Come Out of Your Den   31
Free Tag 17
French Blindman's Buff 76
Fruit Basket, I, II 116

Game, The 105
Geography 96
Ghost 103
Go Last, or Teacher, I, II 36
Going to Jerusalem, or Musical
  Chairs, I, II 117
Good Morning 84
Grand Mammy Tipsy Toe 112
Guard the Chair, I, II 60
Guard the Gate 44, 61
Guessing Songs 102
Guggenheim, or Vocabulary 87

Hand to Hand Race 74
Hang Tag 18
Hands Up 77
Hare and Hounds 72
Hasto Beano 82
Have You Seen My Sheep?, I, II 18
Hide and Seek 72
Hide and Seek in Couples 72
Hide the Clock 82
Hide the Thimble 82
Hiding Game 89
Higher Than the Ground 19
Hip 19
Hoop Rolling 66
Hop O' My Hat 33
Hopping over Bean Bags 32
Hopping Race 32
Hopping Tag, I, II 31
Hopscotch:
  General Rules for Hopscotch 23
  Halfway, I, II 27
  Home 25
  Japanese Ladder 23
  Sky Blue 27
  Wheel 26
  Window, I, II, III 24
Horseshoe Pitching 42
Hot Potato 37
Hound and Rabbits, I, II 21
How Do You Like It? 100
How Do You Like Your Neighbor?   117
How Is It Like Me? 97
Huckle Buckle Bean Stalk 81
Hul-Gul 121

I'm Thinking of a Word, or Crambo   98
I'm Thinking of Something 87
I Give You a Dog 101

PAGE

I Have a Little Dog 21
I See Red, I, II 85
I Send 12
I Spy, I, II 81
Indians Running 83
Interpreting Rhythms, I, II, III, IV
  V 85
Is It Far to Timbuktu? 16

Jack Be Nimble 32
Jackknife Baseball 122
Jackstones 54
Jacob and Rachel, I, II, III 78
Jerusalem, Jericho 114
Jim Blows Out 19
Jingle the Keys 79
Jumping over the Brook 33
Jumping Hurdles 32
Jumping Rope, I, II, III, IV, V 30
Jumping Squares, I, II 28
Jump the Shot 32

Keep Away 36
Keep Ball 35
Kick the Can, or Throw the Stick   69
Knocking 78

Lame Fox 31
Last Couple Out 11
Letter Puzzles 94

Magician 15
Magic Music 85
Mark the Corner 67
Master of the Ring 32
Matching Cards for Partners 122
Midnight 112
Mother Cary's Chickens, I, II 17
Mother Cary's Chickens Dodge Ball   61
Mother, Mother, the Teakettle Is
  Boiling Over 111
Moving Day 118
Mumblety-peg 123
Multiplication Table 50
Murderer, I, II 97
Musical Chairs, or Going to
  Jerusalem 117
My Father Keeps a Grocery Store   99
My Grandmother Doesn't Like Tea   108
My Ship Is Coming from London 102
Mystery Man 85

Name Six 99
Newspaper March 118
New York, I, II 106
Nouns 91

PAGE

Numbers Change, I, II................ 116
Numbers Change in Couples.......... 13
Numbers Change in Line............... 120
Number Target 42

Observation 84
Ocean Wave 118
O'Leary 48
Old Mother Witch, I, II.............. 113
One, Two, Three, Roll................ 46
Orchestra 94
Over Bridges and Roads.............. 7

Parcel Post 116
Pass the Bean Bag...................... 77
Pass the Pebble.......................... 19
Peddler 80
Photography 109
Pies 14
Piggie in the Hole...................... 63
Piggie Move Up.......................... 65
Pin Ball 62
Poets 87
Poison 118
Poison Snake, I, II...................... 58
Polite Conversation 98
Pom Pom Pullaway...................... 16
Potato Race, I, II........................ 75
Predicament 99
Prince of Paris, The.................... 95
Prisoner's Base 8
Prove It 14
Prove It in Colors....................... 15
Proverbs 96
Pussy Wants a Corner.................. 120

Queen Dido Is Dead.................... 121
Quick Numbers 95

Rattlesnake 121
Recognition 100
Red Light, or Cheese It, I, II....... 115
Red Rover 59
Rhymes 95
Rhythm 104
Ring on a String......................... 81
Robber 21
Robbers 73
Roll Over and Back..................... 37
Roly Poly, I, II, III, IV............... 52
Rooster Fight 32
Rope Relay 75
Run Old Bear.............................. 22
Run Sheep Run........................... 70

Sardines 67

PAGE

Save a Friend Tag....................... 12
Schuster, Schuster 80
Sewing Up the Gaps.................... 13
Shadow Tag 19
Sheep in My Pen, or Beckon, I, II 69
Shinny 64
Shooting Gallery 44
Silent Circle, or Beckon............... 76
Singing Proverbs 96
Singing Syllables 99
Skipping Rope 31
Skits and Songs........................... 107
Slap Tag 18
Snatch the Handkerchief.............. 10
Spell Down 92
Spelling Baseball 91
Spin the Platter 120
Squirrels in Trees........................ 118
Stage Coach 102
Stealing Sticks 9
Stick's Up 60
Stiff Legged Tag.......................... 13
Still Pond 76
Stillwater 70
Stock Exchange, or Cross Word
  Game 93
Stone Teacher 80
Stone Witch 20
Stoop Tag, or Black and White
  Stoop Tag, I, II........................ 20
Stop 44
Straddle Ball 18
Suitcase Race 75
Swat 65

Tag in a Circle............................ 19
Tangled Sentences 93
Teacher on the Steps................... 37
Teacher, or Go Last, I, II............ 36
Teakettle 93
Telegrams 98
The Game 105
Tin 14
Tip Cat, I, II, III........................ 63
This, This One, That, That One.... 108
Three Deep 10
Throwing Cards 47
Throwing Light 87
Throw into a Box......................... 46
Throw the Stick, or Kick the Can.. 69
Transformation 95
Travelers, I, II, III...................... 80
Treasure Hunt, I, II, III.............. 70
Trip to Europe, A........................ 108
Twenty Questions 96

PAGE

Two Deep 10

Up Jenkins 78

Vocabulary, or Guggenheim............. 87
Volley Baseball 60, 63

Wall Ball 51
Wall Baseball 38
Wander Ball 37
War 58
War Target 40
Washington Tag 67

PAGE

What Is My Thought Like?............ 98
When I Go to California................. 102
When My Ship Comes In................. 103
Which One? 108
Whistle Talk 84
"White Elephant" Christmas Party 122
Who Am I?.. 86
Who's Got the Ball?....................... 34
Who Started the Motion?............... 84
Wink 116
Wireless 109
Wolf 68

A CATALOG OF SELECTED
DOVER BOOKS
IN ALL FIELDS OF INTEREST

A CATALOG OF SELECTED DOVER
BOOKS IN ALL FIELDS OF INTEREST

DRAWINGS OF REMBRANDT, edited by Seymour Slive. Updated Lippmann, Hofstede de Groot edition, with definitive scholarly apparatus. All portraits, biblical sketches, landscapes, nudes. Oriental figures, classical studies, together with selection of work by followers. 550 illustrations. Total of 630pp. 9⅛ × 12¼.
21485-0, 21486-9 Pa., Two-vol. set $25.00

GHOST AND HORROR STORIES OF AMBROSE BIERCE, Ambrose Bierce. 24 tales vividly imagined, strangely prophetic, and decades ahead of their time in technical skill: "The Damned Thing," "An Inhabitant of Carcosa," "The Eyes of the Panther," "Moxon's Master," and 20 more. 199pp. 5⅜ × 8½. 20767-6 Pa. $3.95

ETHICAL WRITINGS OF MAIMONIDES, Maimonides. Most significant ethical works of great medieval sage, newly translated for utmost precision, readability. Laws Concerning Character Traits, Eight Chapters, more. 192pp. 5⅜ × 8½.
24522-5 Pa. $4.50

THE EXPLORATION OF THE COLORADO RIVER AND ITS CANYONS, J. W. Powell. Full text of Powell's 1,000-mile expedition down the fabled Colorado in 1869. Superb account of terrain, geology, vegetation, Indians, famine, mutiny, treacherous rapids, mighty canyons, during exploration of last unknown part of continental U.S. 400pp. 5⅜ × 8½. 20094-9 Pa. $6.95

HISTORY OF PHILOSOPHY, Julián Marías. Clearest one-volume history on the market. Every major philosopher and dozens of others, to Existentialism and later. 505pp. 5⅜ × 8½. 21739-6 Pa. $8.50

ALL ABOUT LIGHTNING, Martin A. Uman. Highly readable non-technical survey of nature and causes of lightning, thunderstorms, ball lightning, St. Elmo's Fire, much more. Illustrated. 192pp. 5⅜ × 8½. 25237-X Pa. $5.95

SAILING ALONE AROUND THE WORLD, Captain Joshua Slocum. First man to sail around the world, alone, in small boat. One of great feats of seamanship told in delightful manner. 67 illustrations. 294pp. 5⅜ × 8½. 20326-3 Pa. $4.95

LETTERS AND NOTES ON THE MANNERS, CUSTOMS AND CONDITIONS OF THE NORTH AMERICAN INDIANS, George Catlin. Classic account of life among Plains Indians: ceremonies, hunt, warfare, etc. 312 plates. 572pp. of text. 6⅛ × 9¼. 22118-0, 22119-9 Pa. Two-vol. set $15.90

ALASKA: The Harriman Expedition, 1899, John Burroughs, John Muir, et al. Informative, engrossing accounts of two-month, 9,000-mile expedition. Native peoples, wildlife, forests, geography, salmon industry, glaciers, more. Profusely illustrated. 240 black-and-white line drawings. 124 black-and-white photographs. 3 maps. Index. 576pp. 5⅜ × 8½. 25109-8 Pa. $11.95

THE BOOK OF BEASTS: Being a Translation from a Latin Bestiary of the Twelfth Century, T. H. White. Wonderful catalog real and fanciful beasts: manticore, griffin, phoenix, amphivius, jaculus, many more. White's witty erudite commentary on scientific, historical aspects. Fascinating glimpse of medieval mind. Illustrated. 296pp. 5⅜ × 8¼. (Available in U.S. only) 24609-4 Pa. $5.95

FRANK LLOYD WRIGHT: ARCHITECTURE AND NATURE With 160 Illustrations, Donald Hoffmann. Profusely illustrated study of influence of nature—especially prairie—on Wright's designs for Fallingwater, Robie House, Guggenheim Museum, other masterpieces. 96pp. 9¼ × 10¾. 25098-9 Pa. $7.95

FRANK LLOYD WRIGHT'S FALLINGWATER, Donald Hoffmann. Wright's famous waterfall house: planning and construction of organic idea. History of site, owners, Wright's personal involvement. Photographs of various stages of building. Preface by Edgar Kaufmann, Jr. 100 illustrations. 112pp. 9¼ × 10. 23671-4 Pa. $7.95

YEARS WITH FRANK LLOYD WRIGHT: Apprentice to Genius, Edgar Tafel. Insightful memoir by a former apprentice presents a revealing portrait of Wright the man, the inspired teacher, the greatest American architect. 372 black-and-white illustrations. Preface. Index. vi + 228pp. 8¼ × 11. 24801-1 Pa. $9.95

THE STORY OF KING ARTHUR AND HIS KNIGHTS, Howard Pyle. Enchanting version of King Arthur fable has delighted generations with imaginative narratives of exciting adventures and unforgettable illustrations by the author. 41 illustrations. xviii + 313pp. 6⅛ × 9¼. 21445-1 Pa. $6.50

THE GODS OF THE EGYPTIANS, E. A. Wallis Budge. Thorough coverage of numerous gods of ancient Egypt by foremost Egyptologist. Information on evolution of cults, rites and gods; the cult of Osiris; the Book of the Dead and its rites; the sacred animals and birds; Heaven and Hell; and more. 956pp. 6⅛ × 9¼. 22055-9, 22056-7 Pa., Two-vol. set $20.00

A THEOLOGICO-POLITICAL TREATISE, Benedict Spinoza. Also contains unfinished *Political Treatise*. Great classic on religious liberty, theory of government on common consent. R. Elwes translation. Total of 421pp. 5⅜ × 8½. 20249-6 Pa. $6.95

INCIDENTS OF TRAVEL IN CENTRAL AMERICA, CHIAPAS, AND YUCATAN, John L. Stephens. Almost single-handed discovery of Maya culture; exploration of ruined cities, monuments, temples; customs of Indians. 115 drawings. 892pp. 5⅜ × 8½. 22404-X, 22405-8 Pa., Two-vol. set $15.90

LOS CAPRICHOS, Francisco Goya. 80 plates of wild, grotesque monsters and caricatures. Prado manuscript included. 183pp. 6⅝ × 9⅜. 22384-1 Pa. $4.95

AUTOBIOGRAPHY: The Story of My Experiments with Truth, Mohandas K. Gandhi. Not hagiography, but Gandhi in his own words. Boyhood, legal studies, purification, the growth of the Satyagraha (nonviolent protest) movement. Critical, inspiring work of the man who freed India. 480pp. 5⅜ × 8½. (Available in U.S. only) 24593-4 Pa. $6.95

ILLUSTRATED DICTIONARY OF HISTORIC ARCHITECTURE, edited by Cyril M. Harris. Extraordinary compendium of clear, concise definitions for over 5,000 important architectural terms complemented by over 2,000 line drawings. Covers full spectrum of architecture from ancient ruins to 20th-century Modernism. Preface. 592pp. 7½ × 9⅝. 24444-X Pa. $14.95

THE NIGHT BEFORE CHRISTMAS, Clement Moore. Full text, and woodcuts from original 1848 book. Also critical, historical material. 19 illustrations. 40pp. 4⅝ × 6. 22797-9 Pa. $2.25

THE LESSON OF JAPANESE ARCHITECTURE: 165 Photographs, Jiro Harada. Memorable gallery of 165 photographs taken in the 1930's of exquisite Japanese homes of the well-to-do and historic buildings. 13 line diagrams. 192pp. 8⅜ × 11¼. 24778-3 Pa. $8.95

THE AUTOBIOGRAPHY OF CHARLES DARWIN AND SELECTED LETTERS, edited by Francis Darwin. The fascinating life of eccentric genius composed of an intimate memoir by Darwin (intended for his children); commentary by his son, Francis; hundreds of fragments from notebooks, journals, papers; and letters to and from Lyell, Hooker, Huxley, Wallace and Henslow. xi + 365pp. 5⅜ × 8. 20479-0 Pa. $6.95

WONDERS OF THE SKY: Observing Rainbows, Comets, Eclipses, the Stars and Other Phenomena, Fred Schaaf. Charming, easy-to-read poetic guide to all manner of celestial events visible to the naked eye. Mock suns, glories, Belt of Venus, more. Illustrated. 299pp. 5¼ × 8¼. 24402-4 Pa. $7.95

BURNHAM'S CELESTIAL HANDBOOK, Robert Burnham, Jr. Thorough guide to the stars beyond our solar system. Exhaustive treatment. Alphabetical by constellation: Andromeda to Cetus in Vol. 1; Chamaeleon to Orion in Vol. 2; and Pavo to Vulpecula in Vol. 3. Hundreds of illustrations. Index in Vol. 3. 2,000pp. 6⅛ × 9¼. 23567-X, 23568-8, 23673-0 Pa., Three-vol. set $38.85

STAR NAMES: Their Lore and Meaning, Richard Hinckley Allen. Fascinating history of names various cultures have given to constellations and literary and folkloristic uses that have been made of stars. Indexes to subjects. Arabic and Greek names. Biblical references. Bibliography. 563pp. 5⅜ × 8½. 21079-0 Pa. $7.95

THIRTY YEARS THAT SHOOK PHYSICS: The Story of Quantum Theory, George Gamow. Lucid, accessible introduction to influential theory of energy and matter. Careful explanations of Dirac's anti-particles, Bohr's model of the atom, much more. 12 plates. Numerous drawings. 240pp. 5⅜ × 8½. 24895-X Pa. $4.95

CHINESE DOMESTIC FURNITURE IN PHOTOGRAPHS AND MEASURED DRAWINGS, Gustav Ecke. A rare volume, now affordably priced for antique collectors, furniture buffs and art historians. Detailed review of styles ranging from early Shang to late Ming. Unabridged republication. 161 black-and-white drawings, photos. Total of 224pp. 8⅜ × 11¼. (Available in U.S. only) 25171-3 Pa. $12.95

VINCENT VAN GOGH: A Biography, Julius Meier-Graefe. Dynamic, penetrating study of artist's life, relationship with brother, Theo, painting techniques, travels, more. Readable, engrossing. 160pp. 5⅜ × 8½. (Available in U.S. only) 25253-1 Pa. $3.95

HOW TO WRITE, Gertrude Stein. Gertrude Stein claimed anyone could understand her unconventional writing—here are clues to help. Fascinating improvisations, language experiments, explanations illuminate Stein's craft and the art of writing. Total of 414pp. 4⅝ × 6⅜. 23144-5 Pa. $5.95

ADVENTURES AT SEA IN THE GREAT AGE OF SAIL: Five Firsthand Narratives, edited by Elliot Snow. Rare true accounts of exploration, whaling, shipwreck, fierce natives, trade, shipboard life, more. 33 illustrations. Introduction. 353pp. 5⅜ × 8½. 25177-2 Pa. $7.95

THE HERBAL OR GENERAL HISTORY OF PLANTS, John Gerard. Classic descriptions of about 2,850 plants—with over 2,700 illustrations—includes Latin and English names, physical descriptions, varieties, time and place of growth, more. 2,706 illustrations. xlv + 1,678pp. 8½ × 12¼. 23147-X Cloth. $75.00

DOROTHY AND THE WIZARD IN OZ, L. Frank Baum. Dorothy and the Wizard visit the center of the Earth, where people are vegetables, glass houses grow and Oz characters reappear. Classic sequel to *Wizard of Oz*. 256pp. 5⅜ × 8. 24714-7 Pa. $4.95

SONGS OF EXPERIENCE: Facsimile Reproduction with 26 Plates in Full Color, William Blake. This facsimile of Blake's original "Illuminated Book" reproduces 26 full-color plates from a rare 1826 edition. Includes "The Tyger," "London," "Holy Thursday," and other immortal poems. 26 color plates. Printed text of poems. 48pp. 5¼ × 7. 24636-1 Pa. $3.50

SONGS OF INNOCENCE, William Blake. The first and most popular of Blake's famous "Illuminated Books," in a facsimile edition reproducing all 31 brightly colored plates. Additional printed text of each poem. 64pp. 5¼ × 7. 22764-2 Pa. $3.50

PRECIOUS STONES, Max Bauer. Classic, thorough study of diamonds, rubies, emeralds, garnets, etc.: physical character, occurrence, properties, use, similar topics. 20 plates, 8 in color. 94 figures. 659pp. 6⅛ × 9¼. 21910-0, 21911-9 Pa., Two-vol. set $15.90

ENCYCLOPEDIA OF VICTORIAN NEEDLEWORK, S. F. A. Caulfeild and Blanche Saward. Full, precise descriptions of stitches, techniques for dozens of needlecrafts—most exhaustive reference of its kind. Over 800 figures. Total of 679pp. 8⅛ × 11. Two volumes. Vol. 1 22800-2 Pa. $11.95
Vol. 2 22801-0 Pa. $11.95

THE MARVELOUS LAND OF OZ, L. Frank Baum. Second Oz book, the Scarecrow and Tin Woodman are back with hero named Tip, Oz magic. 136 illustrations. 287pp. 5⅜ × 8½. 20692-0 Pa. $5.95

WILD FOWL DECOYS, Joel Barber. Basic book on the subject, by foremost authority and collector. Reveals history of decoy making and rigging, place in American culture, different kinds of decoys, how to make them, and how to use them. 140 plates. 156pp. 7⅞ × 10¾. 20011-6 Pa. $8.95

HISTORY OF LACE, Mrs. Bury Palliser. Definitive, profusely illustrated chronicle of lace from earliest times to late 19th century. Laces of Italy, Greece, England, France, Belgium, etc. Landmark of needlework scholarship. 266 illustrations. 672pp. 6⅛ × 9¼. 24742-2 Pa. $14.95

ILLUSTRATED GUIDE TO SHAKER FURNITURE, Robert Meader. All furniture and appurtenances, with much on unknown local styles. 235 photos. 146pp. 9 × 12. 22819-3 Pa. $7.95

WHALE SHIPS AND WHALING: A Pictorial Survey, George Francis Dow. Over 200 vintage engravings, drawings, photographs of barks, brigs, cutters, other vessels. Also harpoons, lances, whaling guns, many other artifacts. Comprehensive text by foremost authority. 207 black-and-white illustrations. 288pp. 6 × 9. 24808-9 Pa. $8.95

THE BERTRAMS, Anthony Trollope. Powerful portrayal of blind self-will and thwarted ambition includes one of Trollope's most heartrending love stories. 497pp. 5⅜ × 8½. 25119-5 Pa. $8.95

ADVENTURES WITH A HAND LENS, Richard Headstrom. Clearly written guide to observing and studying flowers and grasses, fish scales, moth and insect wings, egg cases, buds, feathers, seeds, leaf scars, moss, molds, ferns, common crystals, etc.—all with an ordinary, inexpensive magnifying glass. 209 exact line drawings aid in your discoveries. 220pp. 5⅜ × 8½. 23330-8 Pa. $3.95

RODIN ON ART AND ARTISTS, Auguste Rodin. Great sculptor's candid, wide-ranging comments on meaning of art; great artists; relation of sculpture to poetry, painting, music; philosophy of life, more. 76 superb black-and-white illustrations of Rodin's sculpture, drawings and prints. 119pp. 8⅜ × 11¼. 24487-3 Pa. $6.95

FIFTY CLASSIC FRENCH FILMS, 1912–1982: A Pictorial Record, Anthony Slide. Memorable stills from Grand Illusion, Beauty and the Beast, Hiroshima, Mon Amour, many more. Credits, plot synopses, reviews, etc. 160pp. 8¼ × 11. 25256-6 Pa. $11.95

THE PRINCIPLES OF PSYCHOLOGY, William James. Famous long course complete, unabridged. Stream of thought, time perception, memory, experimental methods; great work decades ahead of its time. 94 figures. 1,391pp. 5⅜ × 8½. 20381-6, 20382-4 Pa., Two-vol. set $19.90

BODIES IN A BOOKSHOP, R. T. Campbell. Challenging mystery of blackmail and murder with ingenious plot and superbly drawn characters. In the best tradition of British suspense fiction. 192pp. 5⅜ × 8½. 24720-1 Pa. $3.95

CALLAS: PORTRAIT OF A PRIMA DONNA, George Jellinek. Renowned commentator on the musical scene chronicles incredible career and life of the most controversial, fascinating, influential operatic personality of our time. 64 black-and-white photographs. 416pp. 5⅜ × 8¼. 25047-4 Pa. $7.95

GEOMETRY, RELATIVITY AND THE FOURTH DIMENSION, Rudolph Rucker. Exposition of fourth dimension, concepts of relativity as Flatland characters continue adventures. Popular, easily followed yet accurate, profound. 141 illustrations. 133pp. 5⅜ × 8½. 23400-2 Pa. $3.95

HOUSEHOLD STORIES BY THE BROTHERS GRIMM, with pictures by Walter Crane. 53 classic stories—Rumpelstiltskin, Rapunzel, Hansel and Gretel, the Fisherman and his Wife, Snow White, Tom Thumb, Sleeping Beauty, Cinderella, and so much more—lavishly illustrated with original 19th century drawings. 114 illustrations. x + 269pp. 5⅜ × 8½. 21080-4 Pa. $4.50

CATALOG OF DOVER BOOKS

SUNDIALS, Albert Waugh. Far and away the best, most thorough coverage of ideas, mathematics concerned, types, construction, adjusting anywhere. Over 100 illustrations. 230pp. 5⅜ × 8½. 22947-5 Pa. $4.50

PICTURE HISTORY OF THE NORMANDIE: With 190 Illustrations, Frank O. Braynard. Full story of legendary French ocean liner: Art Deco interiors, design innovations, furnishings, celebrities, maiden voyage, tragic fire, much more. Extensive text. 144pp. 8⅞ × 11¾. 25257-4 Pa. $9.95

THE FIRST AMERICAN COOKBOOK: A Facsimile of "American Cookery," 1796, Amelia Simmons. Facsimile of the first American-written cookbook published in the United States contains authentic recipes for colonial favorites—pumpkin pudding, winter squash pudding, spruce beer, Indian slapjacks, and more. Introductory Essay and Glossary of colonial cooking terms. 80pp. 5⅜ × 8½. 24710-4 Pa. $3.50

101 PUZZLES IN THOUGHT AND LOGIC, C. R. Wylie, Jr. Solve murders and robberies, find out which fishermen are liars, how a blind man could possibly identify a color—purely by your own reasoning! 107pp. 5⅜ × 8½. 20367-0 Pa. $2.50

THE BOOK OF WORLD-FAMOUS MUSIC—CLASSICAL, POPULAR AND FOLK, James J. Fuld. Revised and enlarged republication of landmark work in musico-bibliography. Full information about nearly 1,000 songs and compositions including first lines of music and lyrics. New supplement. Index. 800pp. 5⅜ × 8¼. 24857-7 Pa. $14.95

ANTHROPOLOGY AND MODERN LIFE, Franz Boas. Great anthropologist's classic treatise on race and culture. Introduction by Ruth Bunzel. Only inexpensive paperback edition. 255pp. 5⅜ × 8½. 25245-0 Pa. $5.95

THE TALE OF PETER RABBIT, Beatrix Potter. The inimitable Peter's terrifying adventure in Mr. McGregor's garden, with all 27 wonderful, full-color Potter illustrations. 55pp. 4¼ × 5½. (Available in U.S. only) 22827-4 Pa. $1.75

THREE PROPHETIC SCIENCE FICTION NOVELS, H. G. Wells. *When the Sleeper Wakes, A Story of the Days to Come* and *The Time Machine* (full version). 335pp. 5⅜ × 8½. (Available in U.S. only) 20605-X Pa. $5.95

APICIUS COOKERY AND DINING IN IMPERIAL ROME, edited and translated by Joseph Dommers Vehling. Oldest known cookbook in existence offers readers a clear picture of what foods Romans ate, how they prepared them, etc. 49 illustrations. 301pp. 6⅛ × 9¼. 23563-7 Pa. $6.50

SHAKESPEARE LEXICON AND QUOTATION DICTIONARY, Alexander Schmidt. Full definitions, locations, shades of meaning of every word in plays and poems. More than 50,000 exact quotations. 1,485pp. 6½ × 9¼. 22726-X, 22727-8 Pa., Two-vol. set $27.90

THE WORLD'S GREAT SPEECHES, edited by Lewis Copeland and Lawrence W. Lamm. Vast collection of 278 speeches from Greeks to 1970. Powerful and effective models; unique look at history. 842pp. 5⅜ × 8½. 20468-5 Pa. $11.95

CATALOG OF DOVER BOOKS

THE BLUE FAIRY BOOK, Andrew Lang. The first, most famous collection, with many familiar tales: Little Red Riding Hood, Aladdin and the Wonderful Lamp, Puss in Boots, Sleeping Beauty, Hansel and Gretel, Rumpelstiltskin; 37 in all. 138 illustrations. 390pp. 5⅜ × 8½. 21437-0 Pa. $5.95

THE STORY OF THE CHAMPIONS OF THE ROUND TABLE, Howard Pyle. Sir Launcelot, Sir Tristram and Sir Percival in spirited adventures of love and triumph retold in Pyle's inimitable style. 50 drawings, 31 full-page. xviii + 329pp. 6½ × 9¼. 21883-X Pa. $6.95

AUDUBON AND HIS JOURNALS, Maria Audubon. Unmatched two-volume portrait of the great artist, naturalist and author contains his journals, an excellent biography by his granddaughter, expert annotations by the noted ornithologist, Dr. Elliott Coues, and 37 superb illustrations. Total of 1,200pp. 5⅜ × 8.
Vol. I 25143-8 Pa. $8.95
Vol. II 25144-6 Pa. $8.95

GREAT DINOSAUR HUNTERS AND THEIR DISCOVERIES, Edwin H. Colbert. Fascinating, lavishly illustrated chronicle of dinosaur research, 1820's to 1960. Achievements of Cope, Marsh, Brown, Buckland, Mantell, Huxley, many others. 384pp. 5¼ × 8¼. 24701-5 Pa. $6.95

THE TASTEMAKERS, Russell Lynes. Informal, illustrated social history of American taste 1850's–1950's. First popularized categories Highbrow, Lowbrow, Middlebrow. 129 illustrations. New (1979) afterword. 384pp. 6 × 9.
23993-4 Pa. $6.95

DOUBLE CROSS PURPOSES, Ronald A. Knox. A treasure hunt in the Scottish Highlands, an old map, unidentified corpse, surprise discoveries keep reader guessing in this cleverly intricate tale of financial skullduggery. 2 black-and-white maps. 320pp. 5⅜ × 8½. (Available in U.S. only) 25032-6 Pa. $5.95

AUTHENTIC VICTORIAN DECORATION AND ORNAMENTATION IN FULL COLOR: 46 Plates from "Studies in Design," Christopher Dresser. Superb full-color lithographs reproduced from rare original portfolio of a major Victorian designer. 48pp. 9¼ × 12¼. 25083-0 Pa. $7.95

PRIMITIVE ART, Franz Boas. Remains the best text ever prepared on subject, thoroughly discussing Indian, African, Asian, Australian, and, especially, Northern American primitive art. Over 950 illustrations show ceramics, masks, totem poles, weapons, textiles, paintings, much more. 376pp. 5⅜ × 8. 20025-6 Pa. $6.95

SIDELIGHTS ON RELATIVITY, Albert Einstein. Unabridged republication of two lectures delivered by the great physicist in 1920–21. *Ether and Relativity* and *Geometry and Experience*. Elegant ideas in non-mathematical form, accessible to intelligent layman. vi + 56pp. 5⅜ × 8½. 24511-X Pa. $2.95

THE WIT AND HUMOR OF OSCAR WILDE, edited by Alvin Redman. More than 1,000 ripostes, paradoxes, wisecracks: Work is the curse of the drinking classes, I can resist everything except temptation, etc. 258pp. 5⅜ × 8½. 20602-5 Pa. $4.50

ADVENTURES WITH A MICROSCOPE, Richard Headstrom. 59 adventures with clothing fibers, protozoa, ferns and lichens, roots and leaves, much more. 142 illustrations. 232pp. 5⅜ × 8½. 23471-1 Pa. $3.95

PLANTS OF THE BIBLE, Harold N. Moldenke and Alma L. Moldenke. Standard reference to all 230 plants mentioned in Scriptures. Latin name, biblical reference, uses, modern identity, much more. Unsurpassed encyclopedic resource for scholars, botanists, nature lovers, students of Bible. Bibliography. Indexes. 123 black-and-white illustrations. 384pp. 6 × 9. 25069-5 Pa. $8.95

FAMOUS AMERICAN WOMEN: A Biographical Dictionary from Colonial Times to the Present, Robert McHenry, ed. From Pocahontas to Rosa Parks, 1,035 distinguished American women documented in separate biographical entries. Accurate, up-to-date data, numerous categories, spans 400 years. Indices. 493pp. 6½ × 9¼. 24523-3 Pa. $9.95

THE FABULOUS INTERIORS OF THE GREAT OCEAN LINERS IN HISTORIC PHOTOGRAPHS, William H. Miller, Jr. Some 200 superb photographs capture exquisite interiors of world's great "floating palaces"—1890's to 1980's: *Titanic, Ile de France, Queen Elizabeth, United States, Europa,* more. Approx. 200 black-and-white photographs. Captions. Text. Introduction. 160pp. 8⅞ × 11¾. 24756-2 Pa. $9.95

THE GREAT LUXURY LINERS, 1927-1954: A Photographic Record, William H. Miller, Jr. Nostalgic tribute to heyday of ocean liners. 186 photos of Ile de France, Normandie, Leviathan, Queen Elizabeth, United States, many others. Interior and exterior views. Introduction. Captions. 160pp. 9 × 12. 24056-8 Pa. $9.95

A NATURAL HISTORY OF THE DUCKS, John Charles Phillips. Great landmark of ornithology offers complete detailed coverage of nearly 200 species and subspecies of ducks: gadwall, sheldrake, merganser, pintail, many more. 74 full-color plates, 102 black-and-white. Bibliography. Total of 1,920pp. 8⅝ × 11¼. 25141-1, 25142-X Cloth. Two-vol. set $100.00

THE SEAWEED HANDBOOK: An Illustrated Guide to Seaweeds from North Carolina to Canada, Thomas F. Lee. Concise reference covers 78 species. Scientific and common names, habitat, distribution, more. Finding keys for easy identification. 224pp. 5⅜ × 8½. 25215-9 Pa. $5.95

THE TEN BOOKS OF ARCHITECTURE: The 1755 Leoni Edition, Leon Battista Alberti. Rare classic helped introduce the glories of ancient architecture to the Renaissance. 68 black-and-white plates. 336pp. 8⅜ × 11¼. 25239-6 Pa. $14.95

MISS MACKENZIE, Anthony Trollope. Minor masterpieces by Victorian master unmasks many truths about life in 19th-century England. First inexpensive edition in years. 392pp. 5⅜ × 8½. 25201-9 Pa. $7.95

THE RIME OF THE ANCIENT MARINER, Gustave Doré, Samuel Taylor Coleridge. Dramatic engravings considered by many to be his greatest work. The terrifying space of the open sea, the storms and whirlpools of an unknown ocean, the ice of Antarctica, more—all rendered in a powerful, chilling manner. Full text. 38 plates. 77pp. 9¼ × 12. 22305-1 Pa. $4.95

THE EXPEDITIONS OF ZEBULON MONTGOMERY PIKE, Zebulon Montgomery Pike. Fascinating first-hand accounts (1805-6) of exploration of Mississippi River, Indian wars, capture by Spanish dragoons, much more. 1,088pp. 5⅜ × 8½. 25254-X, 25255-8 Pa. Two-vol. set $23.90

A CONCISE HISTORY OF PHOTOGRAPHY: Third Revised Edition, Helmut Gernsheim. Best one-volume history—camera obscura, photochemistry, daguerreotypes, evolution of cameras, film, more. Also artistic aspects—landscape, portraits, fine art, etc. 281 black-and-white photographs. 26 in color. 176pp. 8⅜ × 11¼. 25128-4 Pa. $12.95

THE DORÉ BIBLE ILLUSTRATIONS, Gustave Doré. 241 detailed plates from the Bible: the Creation scenes, Adam and Eve, Flood, Babylon, battle sequences, life of Jesus, etc. Each plate is accompanied by the verses from the King James version of the Bible. 241pp. 9 × 12. 23004-X Pa. $8.95

HUGGER-MUGGER IN THE LOUVRE, Elliot Paul. Second Homer Evans mystery-comedy. Theft at the Louvre involves sleuth in hilarious, madcap caper. "A knockout."—Books. 336pp. 5⅜ × 8½. 25185-3 Pa. $5.95

FLATLAND, E. A. Abbott. Intriguing and enormously popular science-fiction classic explores the complexities of trying to survive as a two-dimensional being in a three-dimensional world. Amusingly illustrated by the author. 16 illustrations. 103pp. 5⅜ × 8½. 20001-9 Pa. $2.25

THE HISTORY OF THE LEWIS AND CLARK EXPEDITION, Meriwether Lewis and William Clark, edited by Elliott Coues. Classic edition of Lewis and Clark's day-by-day journals that later became the basis for U.S. claims to Oregon and the West. Accurate and invaluable geographical, botanical, biological, meteorological and anthropological material. Total of 1,508pp. 5⅜ × 8½.
21268-8, 21269-6, 21270-X Pa. Three-vol. set $25.50

LANGUAGE, TRUTH AND LOGIC, Alfred J. Ayer. Famous, clear introduction to Vienna, Cambridge schools of Logical Positivism. Role of philosophy, elimination of metaphysics, nature of analysis, etc. 160pp. 5⅜ × 8½. (Available in U.S. and Canada only) 20010-8 Pa. $2.95

MATHEMATICS FOR THE NONMATHEMATICIAN, Morris Kline. Detailed, college-level treatment of mathematics in cultural and historical context, with numerous exercises. For liberal arts students. Preface. Recommended Reading Lists. Tables. Index. Numerous black-and-white figures. xvi + 641pp. 5⅜ × 8½.
24823-2 Pa. $11.95

28 SCIENCE FICTION STORIES, H. G. Wells. Novels, *Star Begotten* and *Men Like Gods*, plus 26 short stories: "Empire of the Ants," "A Story of the Stone Age," "The Stolen Bacillus," "In the Abyss," etc. 915pp. 5⅜ × 8½. (Available in U.S. only)
20265-8 Cloth. $10.95

HANDBOOK OF PICTORIAL SYMBOLS, Rudolph Modley. 3,250 signs and symbols, many systems in full; official or heavy commercial use. Arranged by subject. Most in Pictorial Archive series. 143pp. 8⅛ × 11. 23357-X Pa. $5.95

INCIDENTS OF TRAVEL IN YUCATAN, John L. Stephens. Classic (1843) exploration of jungles of Yucatan, looking for evidences of Maya civilization. Travel adventures, Mexican and Indian culture, etc. Total of 669pp. 5⅜ × 8½.
20926-1, 20927-X Pa., Two-vol. set $9.90

DEGAS: An Intimate Portrait, Ambroise Vollard. Charming, anecdotal memoir by famous art dealer of one of the greatest 19th-century French painters. 14 black-and-white illustrations. Introduction by Harold L. Van Doren. 96pp. 5⅜ × 8½.
25131-4 Pa. $3.95

PERSONAL NARRATIVE OF A PILGRIMAGE TO ALMANDINAH AND MECCAH, Richard Burton. Great travel classic by remarkably colorful personality. Burton, disguised as a Moroccan, visited sacred shrines of Islam, narrowly escaping death. 47 illustrations. 959pp. 5⅜ × 8½.   21217-3, 21218-1 Pa., Two-vol. set $19.90

PHRASE AND WORD ORIGINS, A. H. Holt. Entertaining, reliable, modern study of more than 1,200 colorful words, phrases, origins and histories. Much unexpected information. 254pp. 5⅜ × 8½.   20758-7 Pa. $4.95

THE RED THUMB MARK, R. Austin Freeman. In this first Dr. Thorndyke case, the great scientific detective draws fascinating conclusions from the nature of a single fingerprint. Exciting story, authentic science. 320pp. 5⅜ × 8½. (Available in U.S. only)   25210-8 Pa. $5.95

AN EGYPTIAN HIEROGLYPHIC DICTIONARY, E. A. Wallis Budge. Monumental work containing about 25,000 words or terms that occur in texts ranging from 3000 B.C. to 600 A.D. Each entry consists of a transliteration of the word, the word in hieroglyphs, and the meaning in English. 1,314pp. 6⅜ × 10.
23615-3, 23616-1 Pa., Two-vol. set $27.90

THE COMPLEAT STRATEGYST: Being a Primer on the Theory of Games of Strategy, J. D. Williams. Highly entertaining classic describes, with many illustrated examples, how to select best strategies in conflict situations. Prefaces. Appendices. xvi + 268pp. 5⅜ × 8½.   25101-2 Pa. $5.95

THE ROAD TO OZ, L. Frank Baum. Dorothy meets the Shaggy Man, little Button-Bright and the Rainbow's beautiful daughter in this delightful trip to the magical Land of Oz. 272pp. 5⅜ × 8.   25208-6 Pa. $4.95

POINT AND LINE TO PLANE, Wassily Kandinsky. Seminal exposition of role of point, line, other elements in non-objective painting. Essential to understanding 20th-century art. 127 illustrations. 192pp. 6½ × 9¼.   23808-3 Pa. $4.50

LADY ANNA, Anthony Trollope. Moving chronicle of Countess Lovel's bitter struggle to win for herself and daughter Anna their rightful rank and fortune—perhaps at cost of sanity itself. 384pp. 5⅜ × 8½.   24669-8 Pa. $6.95

EGYPTIAN MAGIC, E. A. Wallis Budge. Sums up all that is known about magic in Ancient Egypt: the role of magic in controlling the gods, powerful amulets that warded off evil spirits, scarabs of immortality, use of wax images, formulas and spells, the secret name, much more. 253pp. 5⅜ × 8½.   22681-6 Pa. $4.00

THE DANCE OF SIVA, Ananda Coomaraswamy. Preeminent authority unfolds the vast metaphysic of India: the revelation of her art, conception of the universe, social organization, etc. 27 reproductions of art masterpieces. 192pp. 5⅜ × 8½.
24817-8 Pa. $5.95

CHRISTMAS CUSTOMS AND TRADITIONS, Clement A. Miles. Origin, evolution, significance of religious, secular practices. Caroling, gifts, yule logs, much more. Full, scholarly yet fascinating; non-sectarian. 400pp. 5⅜ × 8½.
23354-5 Pa. $6.50

THE HUMAN FIGURE IN MOTION, Eadweard Muybridge. More than 4,500 stopped-action photos, in action series, showing undraped men, women, children jumping, lying down, throwing, sitting, wrestling, carrying, etc. 390pp. 7⅞ × 10⅝.
20204-6 Cloth. $21.95

THE MAN WHO WAS THURSDAY, Gilbert Keith Chesterton. Witty, fast-paced novel about a club of anarchists in turn-of-the-century London. Brilliant social, religious, philosophical speculations. 128pp. 5⅜ × 8½. 25121-7 Pa. $3.95

A CEZANNE SKETCHBOOK: Figures, Portraits, Landscapes and Still Lifes, Paul Cezanne. Great artist experiments with tonal effects, light, mass, other qualities in over 100 drawings. A revealing view of developing master painter, precursor of Cubism. 102 black-and-white illustrations. 144pp. 8¾ × 6⅜. 24790-2 Pa. $5.95

AN ENCYCLOPEDIA OF BATTLES: Accounts of Over 1,560 Battles from 1479 B.C. to the Present, David Eggenberger. Presents essential details of every major battle in recorded history, from the first battle of Megiddo in 1479 B.C. to Grenada in 1984. List of Battle Maps. New Appendix covering the years 1967–1984. Index. 99 illustrations. 544pp. 6½ × 9¼. 24913-1 Pa. $14.95

AN ETYMOLOGICAL DICTIONARY OF MODERN ENGLISH, Ernest Weekley. Richest, fullest work, by foremost British lexicographer. Detailed word histories. Inexhaustible. Total of 856pp. 6½ × 9¼.
21873-2, 21874-0 Pa., Two-vol. set $17.00

WEBSTER'S AMERICAN MILITARY BIOGRAPHIES, edited by Robert McHenry. Over 1,000 figures who shaped 3 centuries of American military history. Detailed biographies of Nathan Hale, Douglas MacArthur, Mary Hallaren, others. Chronologies of engagements, more. Introduction. Addenda. 1,033 entries in alphabetical order. xi + 548pp. 6½ × 9¼. (Available in U.S. only)
24758-9 Pa. $11.95

LIFE IN ANCIENT EGYPT, Adolf Erman. Detailed older account, with much not in more recent books: domestic life, religion, magic, medicine, commerce, and whatever else needed for complete picture. Many illustrations. 597pp. 5⅜ × 8½.
22632-8 Pa. $8.50

HISTORIC COSTUME IN PICTURES, Braun & Schneider. Over 1,450 costumed figures shown, covering a wide variety of peoples: kings, emperors, nobles, priests, servants, soldiers, scholars, townsfolk, peasants, merchants, courtiers, cavaliers, and more. 256pp. 8⅜ × 11¼. 23150-X Pa. $7.95

THE NOTEBOOKS OF LEONARDO DA VINCI, edited by J. P. Richter. Extracts from manuscripts reveal great genius; on painting, sculpture, anatomy, sciences, geography, etc. Both Italian and English. 186 ms. pages reproduced, plus 500 additional drawings, including studies for *Last Supper, Sforza* monument, etc. 860pp. 7⅞ × 10¾. (Available in U.S. only) 22572-0, 22573-9 Pa., Two-vol. set $25.90

THE ART NOUVEAU STYLE BOOK OF ALPHONSE MUCHA: All 72 Plates from "Documents Decoratifs" in Original Color, Alphonse Mucha. Rare copyright-free design portfolio by high priest of Art Nouveau. Jewelry, wallpaper, stained glass, furniture, figure studies, plant and animal motifs, etc. Only complete one-volume edition. 80pp. 9⅜ × 12¼.   24044-4 Pa. $8.95

ANIMALS: 1,419 COPYRIGHT-FREE ILLUSTRATIONS OF MAMMALS, BIRDS, FISH, INSECTS, ETC., edited by Jim Harter. Clear wood engravings present, in extremely lifelike poses, over 1,000 species of animals. One of the most extensive pictorial sourcebooks of its kind. Captions. Index. 284pp. 9 × 12.
23766-4 Pa. $9.95

OBELISTS FLY HIGH, C. Daly King. Masterpiece of American detective fiction, long out of print, involves murder on a 1935 transcontinental flight—"a very thrilling story"—NY Times. Unabridged and unaltered republication of the edition published by William Collins Sons & Co. Ltd., London, 1935. 288pp. 5⅜ × 8½. (Available in U.S. only)   25036-9 Pa. $4.95

VICTORIAN AND EDWARDIAN FASHION: A Photographic Survey, Alison Gernsheim. First fashion history completely illustrated by contemporary photographs. Full text plus 235 photos, 1840–1914, in which many celebrities appear. 240pp. 6½ × 9¼.   24205-6 Pa. $6.00

THE ART OF THE FRENCH ILLUSTRATED BOOK, 1700–1914, Gordon N. Ray. Over 630 superb book illustrations by Fragonard, Delacroix, Daumier, Doré, Grandville, Manet, Mucha, Steinlen, Toulouse-Lautrec and many others. Preface. Introduction. 633 halftones. Indices of artists, authors & titles, binders and provenances. Appendices. Bibliography. 608pp. 8⅜ × 11¼.   25086-5 Pa. $24.95

THE WONDERFUL WIZARD OF OZ, L. Frank Baum. Facsimile in full color of America's finest children's classic. 143 illustrations by W. W. Denslow. 267pp. 5⅜ × 8½.   20691-2 Pa. $5.95

FRONTIERS OF MODERN PHYSICS: New Perspectives on Cosmology, Relativity, Black Holes and Extraterrestrial Intelligence, Tony Rothman, et al. For the intelligent layman. Subjects include: cosmological models of the universe; black holes; the neutrino; the search for extraterrestrial intelligence. Introduction. 46 black-and-white illustrations. 192pp. 5⅜ × 8½.   24587-X Pa. $6.95

THE FRIENDLY STARS, Martha Evans Martin & Donald Howard Menzel. Classic text marshalls the stars together in an engaging, non-technical survey, presenting them as sources of beauty in night sky. 23 illustrations. Foreword. 2 star charts. Index. 147pp. 5⅜ × 8½.   21099-5 Pa. $3.50

FADS AND FALLACIES IN THE NAME OF SCIENCE, Martin Gardner. Fair, witty appraisal of cranks, quacks, and quackeries of science and pseudoscience: hollow earth, Velikovsky, orgone energy, Dianetics, flying saucers, Bridey Murphy, food and medical fads, etc. Revised, expanded In the Name of Science. "A very able and even-tempered presentation."—The New Yorker. 363pp. 5⅜ × 8.
20394-8 Pa. $6.50

ANCIENT EGYPT: ITS CULTURE AND HISTORY, J. E Manchip White. From pre-dynastics through Ptolemies: society, history, political structure, religion, daily life, literature, cultural heritage. 48 plates. 217pp. 5⅜ × 8½.   22548-8 Pa. $4.95

SIR HARRY HOTSPUR OF HUMBLETHWAITE, Anthony Trollope. Incisive, unconventional psychological study of a conflict between a wealthy baronet, his idealistic daughter, and their scapegrace cousin. The 1870 novel in its first inexpensive edition in years. 250pp. 5⅜ × 8½.   24953-0 Pa. $5.95

LASERS AND HOLOGRAPHY, Winston E. Kock. Sound introduction to burgeoning field, expanded (1981) for second edition. Wave patterns, coherence, lasers, diffraction, zone plates, properties of holograms, recent advances. 84 illustrations. 160pp. 5⅜ × 8¼. (Except in United Kingdom)   24041-X Pa. $3.50

INTRODUCTION TO ARTIFICIAL INTELLIGENCE: SECOND, EN-LARGED EDITION, Philip C. Jackson, Jr. Comprehensive survey of artificial intelligence—the study of how machines (computers) can be made to act intelligently. Includes introductory and advanced material. Extensive notes updating the main text. 132 black-and-white illustrations. 512pp. 5⅜ × 8½.   24864-X Pa. $8.95

HISTORY OF INDIAN AND INDONESIAN ART, Ananda K. Coomaraswamy. Over 400 illustrations illuminate classic study of Indian art from earliest Harappa finds to early 20th century. Provides philosophical, religious and social insights. 304pp. 6⅜ × 9⅜.   25005-9 Pa. $8.95

THE GOLEM, Gustav Meyrink. Most famous supernatural novel in modern European literature, set in Ghetto of Old Prague around 1890. Compelling story of mystical experiences, strange transformations, profound terror. 13 black-and-white illustrations. 224pp. 5⅜ × 8½. (Available in U.S. only)   25025-3 Pa. $5.95

ARMADALE, Wilkie Collins. Third great mystery novel by the author of *The Woman in White* and *The Moonstone*. Original magazine version with 40 illustrations. 597pp. 5⅜ × 8½.   23429-0 Pa. $9.95

PICTORIAL ENCYCLOPEDIA OF HISTORIC ARCHITECTURAL PLANS, DETAILS AND ELEMENTS: With 1,880 Line Drawings of Arches, Domes, Doorways, Facades, Gables, Windows, etc., John Theodore Haneman. Sourcebook of inspiration for architects, designers, others. Bibliography. Captions. 141pp. 9 × 12.   24605-1 Pa. $6.95

BENCHLEY LOST AND FOUND, Robert Benchley. Finest humor from early 30's, about pet peeves, child psychologists, post office and others. Mostly unavailable elsewhere. 73 illustrations by Peter Arno and others. 183pp. 5⅜ × 8½.
                                                    22410-4 Pa. $3.95

ERTÉ GRAPHICS, Erté. Collection of striking color graphics: *Seasons, Alphabet, Numerals, Aces* and *Precious Stones*. 50 plates, including 4 on covers. 48pp. 9⅜ × 12¼.   23580-7 Pa. $6.95

THE JOURNAL OF HENRY D. THOREAU, edited by Bradford Torrey, F. H. Allen. Complete reprinting of 14 volumes, 1837–61, over two million words; the sourcebooks for *Walden*, etc. Definitive. All original sketches, plus 75 photographs. 1,804pp. 8½ × 12¼.   20312-3, 20313-1 Cloth., Two-vol. set $80.00

CASTLES: THEIR CONSTRUCTION AND HISTORY, Sidney Toy. Traces castle development from ancient roots. Nearly 200 photographs and drawings illustrate moats, keeps, baileys, many other features. Caernarvon, Dover Castles, Hadrian's Wall, Tower of London, dozens more. 256pp. 5⅜ × 8¼.
                                                    24898-4 Pa. $5.95

AMERICAN CLIPPER SHIPS: 1833–1858, Octavius T. Howe & Frederick C. Matthews. Fully-illustrated, encyclopedic review of 352 clipper ships from the period of America's greatest maritime supremacy. Introduction. 109 halftones. 5 black-and-white line illustrations. Index. Total of 928pp. 5⅜ × 8½.
25115-2, 25116-0 Pa., Two-vol. set $17.90

TOWARDS A NEW ARCHITECTURE, Le Corbusier. Pioneering manifesto by great architect, near legendary founder of "International School." Technical and aesthetic theories, views on industry, economics, relation of form to function, "mass-production spirit," much more. Profusely illustrated. Unabridged translation of 13th French edition. Introduction by Frederick Etchells. 320pp. 6⅛ × 9¼. (Available in U.S. only)
25023-7 Pa. $8.95

THE BOOK OF KELLS, edited by Blanche Cirker. Inexpensive collection of 32 full-color, full-page plates from the greatest illuminated manuscript of the Middle Ages, painstakingly reproduced from rare facsimile edition. Publisher's Note. Captions. 32pp. 9⅜ × 12¼.
24345-1 Pa. $4.95

BEST SCIENCE FICTION STORIES OF H. G. WELLS, H. G. Wells. Full novel The Invisible Man, plus 17 short stories: "The Crystal Egg," "Aepyornis Island," "The Strange Orchid," etc. 303pp. 5⅜ × 8½. (Available in U.S. only)
21531-8 Pa. $4.95

AMERICAN SAILING SHIPS: Their Plans and History, Charles G. Davis. Photos, construction details of schooners, frigates, clippers, other sailcraft of 18th to early 20th centuries—plus entertaining discourse on design, rigging, nautical lore, much more. 137 black-and-white illustrations. 240pp. 6⅛ × 9¼.
24658-2 Pa. $5.95

ENTERTAINING MATHEMATICAL PUZZLES, Martin Gardner. Selection of author's favorite conundrums involving arithmetic, money, speed, etc., with lively commentary. Complete solutions. 112pp. 5⅜ × 8½.
25211-6 Pa. $2.95

THE WILL TO BELIEVE, HUMAN IMMORTALITY, William James. Two books bound together. Effect of irrational on logical, and arguments for human immortality. 402pp. 5⅜ × 8½.
20291-7 Pa. $7.50

THE HAUNTED MONASTERY and THE CHINESE MAZE MURDERS, Robert Van Gulik. 2 full novels by Van Gulik continue adventures of Judge Dee and his companions. An evil Taoist monastery, seemingly supernatural events; overgrown topiary maze that hides strange crimes. Set in 7th-century China. 27 illustrations. 328pp. 5⅜ × 8½.
23502-5 Pa. $5.95

CELEBRATED CASES OF JUDGE DEE (DEE GOONG AN), translated by Robert Van Gulik. Authentic 18th-century Chinese detective novel; Dee and associates solve three interlocked cases. Led to Van Gulik's own stories with same characters. Extensive introduction. 9 illustrations. 237pp. 5⅜ × 8½.
23337-5 Pa. $4.95

Prices subject to change without notice.

Available at your book dealer or write for free catalog to Dept. GI, Dover Publications, Inc., 31 East 2nd St., Mineola, N.Y. 11501. Dover publishes more than 175 books each year on science, elementary and advanced mathematics, biology, music, art, literary history, social sciences and other areas.